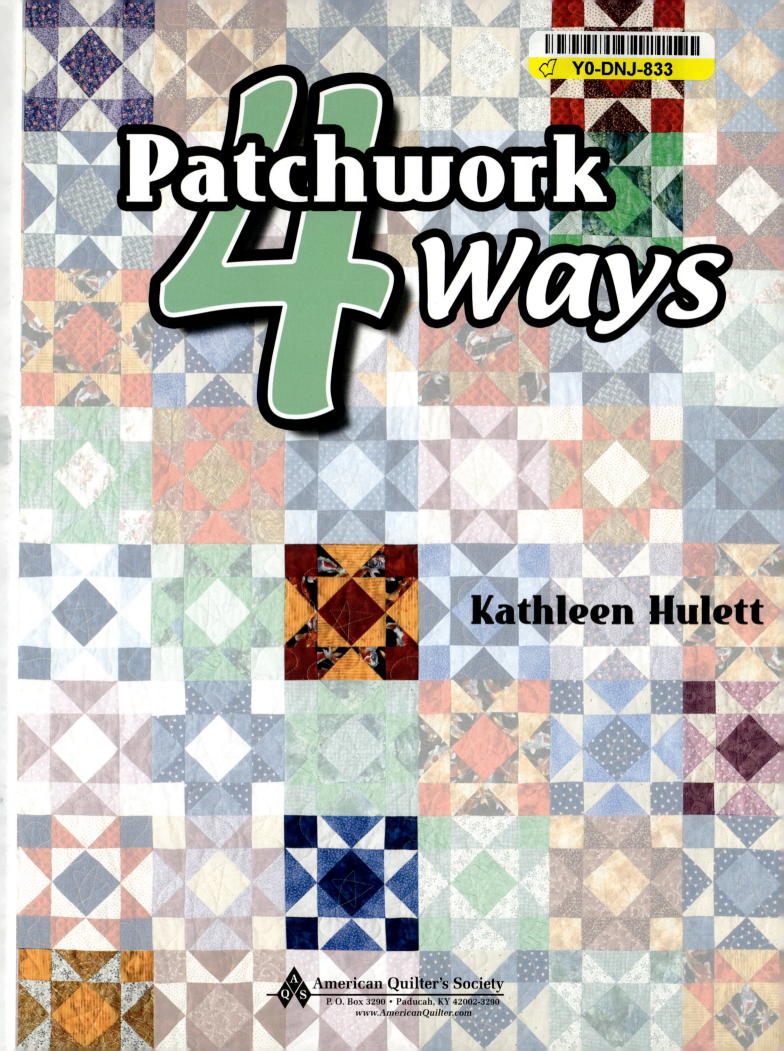

Patchwork
4
Ways

Kathleen Hulett

American Quilter's Society
P. O. Box 3290 • Paducah, KY 42002-3290
www.AmericanQuilter.com

Located in Paducah, Kentucky, the American Quilter's Society (AQS) is dedicated to promoting the accomplishments of today's quilters. Through its publications and events, AQS strives to honor today's quiltmakers and their work and to inspire future creativity and innovation in quiltmaking.

EXECUTIVE BOOK EDITOR: ANDI MILAM REYNOLDS
SENIOR BOOK EDITOR: LINDA BAXTER LASCO
GRAPHIC DESIGN: LYNDA SMITH AND ANGELA SCHADE
ILLUSTRATIONS: LYNDA SMITH AND ELAINE WILSON
COVER DESIGN: MICHAEL BUCKINGHAM
PHOTOGRAPHY: CHARLES R. LYNCH
HOW-TO PHOTOGRAPHY: KATHLEEN HULETT (EXCEPT WHERE NOTED)

Additional copies of this book may be ordered from the American Quilter's Society, PO Box 3290, Paducah, KY 42002-3290, or online at www.AmericanQuilter.com.

Text © 2009, Author, Kathleen Hulett
Artwork © 2009, American Quilter's Society

Library of Congress Cataloging-in-Publication Data

Hulett, Kathleen.
  Patchwork 4 ways / by Kathleen Hulett.
      p. cm.
  ISBN 978-1-57432-997-1
  1. Patchwork–Patterns. I. Title.

TT835.H853 2009
746.46'041–dc22
                                    2009039756

American Quilter's Society
P. O. Box 3290 • Paducah, KY 42002-3290
www.AmericanQuilter.com

Table of Contents

Introduction & General Instructions

The quilts in this book are made with just four easy blocks—a Star block, a Snow Goose block, which resembles a cross between a Flying Geese and Snowball block, a small Log Cabin, and a strip-pieced block that I'll refer to simply as the Stripe block. That's it. All of the quilts in this book are made from a selection of one or more of these blocks, with all of them used in the CABINS IN THE STARS quilt, which was the inspiration for this book.

Instructions for making each of the four blocks are illustrated in the pages preceding the quilt patterns. Refer to them as needed as you piece your quilts. Despite the number of triangles you will see in the quilts, you will not have to cut out any triangles, other than the large setting triangles used in making quilts with an on-point layout. Instead, you will sew diagonally across a square and then cut off the excess fabric to make a triangle shape. While it does waste a bit of fabric, it yields a nice, easy block and you can save the trimmed triangles for another project. Don't throw them away! (See pages 78–79 for some ideas on using the leftovers.)

Instructions for the individual quilts follow the illustration of each quilt. You need only refer back to the basic block instructions to make the blocks. Since the quilts all use the same blocks, it seemed unnecessary to repeat the instructions for each of them. Just as I dislike wasting good fabric, I dislike wasting paper.

If you are one who likes to design or alter patterns, this book includes a special section just for you, too—The Math of Quilting on pages 86-92. In this section instructions and charts will guide you in resizing quilt patterns and calculating fabric needs. I found these charts to be very helpful as I designed the quilts in this book, and I'm confident that you will, too.

Basic Materials

Rotary cutter, ruler, and cutting mat: You can make the quilts without them, but it is so much easier and faster to use rotary-cutting methods to cut your fabric strips. Just be careful to keep your fingers out of the way of the blade—it is razor sharp! If it isn't, it's time to replace it.

Scissors: Even though you'll use your rotary cutter for most cutting, you'll still need a good, sharp pair of scissors to cut threads and trim seam allowances.

Sewing machine with markings for ¼" seam allowance: If your machine does not have a ¼" piecing foot or a mark for a ¼" seam allowance, you can mark the ¼" with masking tape or a permanent marker. Just measure from the center of your needle. Don't assume that your foot is ¼". Check it out to make sure or your quilt blocks will come out shy of the desired measurement.

Needles: A nice sharp needle in your machine is essential. You will also need a hand stitching needle to sew your binding to the back of your quilt.

Iron: You will need to press your blocks and quilt pieces frequently as you assemble them. You can improvise your ironing surface but an iron is essential for sewing.

Pins: Flat-headed pins are nice, but any sharp pins will do. One-inch safety pins are handy for holding your quilt sandwich layers together for quilting. I prefer the bent ones that are made especially for this purpose, but regular ones will do.

Quilt basting spray: Optional, but oh, so helpful for securing the quilt top, batting, and backing together before quilting! The aerosol cans of spray can be found at fabric stores and in the fabric department of some discount stores.

Walking foot: Another optional item, but it makes quilting the quilt and sewing the binding on ever so much easier. It allows the quilt top and the backing to feed through the machine at the same rate and lessens the slippage that can occur otherwise.

General Instructions

Yardage measurements: Yardage requirements are based on 40" of usable fabric, unless noted otherwise (for some backing fabrics). The width of your fabrics will often be two to four inches more than this, but this assumption will allow you plenty of fabric to work with in case of shrinkage. Yardage amounts also allow a bit extra for squaring up crooked ends.

Prewashing fabric: There is some controversy surrounding the need to prewash fabric. I will admit that although I generally recommend prewashing, I don't always do

Patchwork 4 Ways *by Kathleen Hulett*

so. Newer fabrics don't tend to shrink as much as those from days gone by, but there are no guarantees. When in doubt, prewash and dry. Cotton can shrink!

Seam allowances: When piecing your quilt top, all seam allowances are ¼" wide and are generally pressed to one side. If you have done fashion sewing, you may be used to pressing your seam allowances open. Quilt making is different. Pressing to one side strengthens your seam. The rule of thumb is to press toward the dark fabric, but if you must choose between that and pressing toward the side with fewer seams, choose the latter, as it will lessen the bulk in the seam.

Matching seam allowances: You will often need to sew blocks or segments of blocks together where the seams meet. When this is the case, it is very important to make sure that those seams match closely. To accomplish this, press your seam allowances in opposite directions so the seams will butt up against each other (fig. 1). Place a straight pin through the matching seams (fig. 2), then use a second pin to stabilize the pieces for sewing.

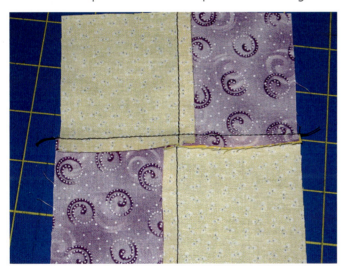

Fig. 1. Press seam allowances in opposite directions.

Fig. 2. Pin match the seams.

Partial Seams

Two quilt assemblies require joining sections with partial seams (TWINKLE, TWINKLE and BUILDING BLOCKS). Adding four same-length strips to a square illustrates the technique. Add strip 1, stopping a bit before the end of the seam (fig 3). Add strips 2, 3, and 4 (fig. 4), then finish the strip 1 seam (fig. 5).

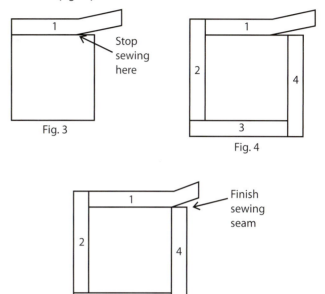

Chain piecing: You will often find that you have many identical blocks, or units of blocks, that need to be pieced. You will save a lot of time and see your results much faster if you chain piece them. What is chain piecing? When sewing more than one set of pieces together, do not cut the thread between them. Instead, once the first set is sewn, place the next set on the machine to sew it without cutting the thread. Keep going until you have sewn all the units you wish to sew (fig. 6). Then cut them apart.

Fig. 6. Chain piecing saves time.

Assembly of the 4 Blocks

All of the quilts in this book are based on four basic blocks. The pieces you will be cutting to make each block are coded by letter, according to their shape and relative size. As you look at the instructions for the blocks, you will see that the parts are assigned a letter according to their shape and position in each block (fig. 1). These letter codes will be used throughout the book.

For example, when cutting a piece labeled B, you will know that it belongs either in the center of a Star block or as the point, or wing, of a Snow Goose block. The sizes will differ depending on the quilt, so pay close attention to the specific cutting instructions given for each quilt. If there are large and small versions of the same block in the same quilt, as in BUILDING BLOCKS and TWINKLE, TWINKLE, the pieces may be coded "lg" or "sm" to designate their intended block.

Code	Shape	Description
A		Large Rectangle – for Snow Goose background
B		Large Square – for Snow Goose triangles (wings) & Star centers
C		Small Square – for Star centers, points & corners – for Log Cabin centers and smallest square
D		Short Rectangle – for Flying Geese segment of Star blocks – for short sides of Log Cabin blocks
E		Long Rectangle – for long sides of Log Cabin block
N		Strip – for outer strips of Stripe block
W		Strip – for center strip of Stripe block

Fig. 1. Quilt piece codes

Patchwork 4 Ways *by Kathleen Hulett*

Star Block Assembly

Each Star block requires:

*One B square and four C squares for the center unit
*Four D rectangles and eight C squares for the Flying Geese (star points)
*Four C squares for the corners

The center units: Make one center for each Star block. Draw a diagonal line from corner to corner on the wrong side (back) of each of the small C squares. Align a square C with one corner of a large square B with right sides together (fig. 2). Sew along the drawn line. Trim the excess, leaving a ¼" seam allowance. Press open, pressing the seam allowance toward the corner.

Fig. 2. Sew the first corner to the center patch.

Tip: When you sew your diagonal seam, sew just a thread width to the outside of the drawn line. When you press the block open, the tiny bit of extra space will compensate for the fold.

Repeat the procedure for the other 3 corners (fig. 3).

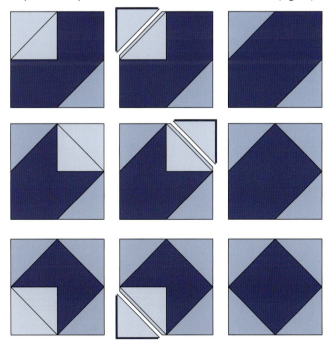

Fig. 3. Sew the remaining squares to the center patch.

The Flying Geese (star points): Make 4 Flying Geese units for each Star block.

Draw a diagonal line from corner to corner on the wrong side (back) of each of the C squares. Align a square C with one end of a rectangle D, right sides together. Sew along the drawn line. Trim the excess, leaving a ¼" seam allowance. Press open, pressing the seam allowance toward the corner. Repeat to complete the Flying Geese unit (fig. 4).

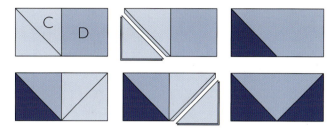

Fig. 4. Sew a square C diagonally to both ends of rectangle D. Make 4.

Measure the finished units of your Star block and trim, if necessary, to the desired size. It's not unusual for some distortion to occur during sewing. Trimming up now will make the final assembly of your block much easier and more accurate.

Final assembly of the Star block

Lay out the 5 pieced units and 4 squares as shown (fig. 5). Join the units in 3 rows. Press all your seam allowances toward the Flying Geese units. Pin carefully where the seams meet and sew these 3 rows together to complete your Star block.

Don't feel badly if your points do not turn out perfectly. It happens to me quite often! The seam ripper is my friend though, and when I can, I'll go back and make adjustments to get it right. If I can't, well...nobody's perfect!

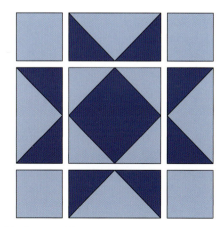

Fig. 5. Star block assembly

Assembly of the 4 Blocks

Tip: To line up the center and Flying Geese points where they meet, place a pin straight through both points. Pin the units together on either side of that pin and remove the center pin. Look for the X created by the seams and sew just a teensy bit to the outside of the center of that X. When done carefully, the points will be ¼" from the edge of your block.

Measure your block and trim to square it up, if necessary. Congratulations. Your Star block is complete!

Log Cabin Block Assembly

The Log Cabin block usually uses 3 colors.
  Each block requires:
    *One center C
    *One C and one D of a second color
    *One D and one E of a third color

The Log Cabin block is sewn by adding pieces around the center of the block in a clockwise or counterclockwise manner, pressing after each addition (fig. 6).

Fig 6. Join the pieces as shown.

Stripe Block Assembly

Strip-piecing for the Stripe block uses N and W strips of fabric. In some patterns these strips are the same width, in others the W strip is wider than the N strips. Your pattern will tell you what width to cut them. Don't worry if the strip lengths are not exactly the same. That will be dealt with later on.

Each Stripe block requires:
    *One W strip
    *Two N strips

Sew a strip N to each side of center strip W (fig. 7). Press carefully so as not to bend your unit into a rainbow shape.

Fig. 7

Cut the strip-set into blocks, according to the size specified in the pattern (fig. 8).

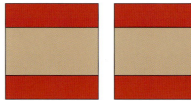

Fig. 8

Snow Goose Block Assembly

I chose to call this block Snow Goose because it resembles both the Flying Geese and Snowball blocks. (The Snowball is not used in this book.) The block is assembled in the same manner as the Flying Geese units.

Each Snow Goose block requires:
    *One A rectangle
    *Two B squares

Draw a diagonal line from corner to corner on the wrong side (back) of each of the B squares. Align a square B with one corner of a rectangle A, right sides together.

Sew along the drawn line. Trim the excess, leaving a ¼" seam allowance. Press open, pressing the seam allowance toward the corner (fig. 9).

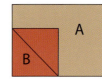

Fig. 9

Repeat to complete the Snow Goose block (fig. 10).

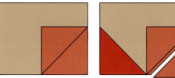

Fig. 10

That's all there is to it. Didn't I tell you that these blocks are simple?

Setting Triangles and Borders

Side and Corner Triangles

Quilts set diagonally, or on point, involve an extra step of cutting and sewing setting and corner triangles to fill in the spaces around the blocks. These are the only triangles you will have to cut for the quilts in this book, but they're big and easy. Really! The cutting charts will give you the dimensions of the squares you will need to start with.

Side setting triangles

To cut the side setting triangles, which will fill in the spaces around the edges of the quilt, cut squares in half diagonally, then cut each of the resulting triangles in half again, as if cutting the square diagonally from the other direction (fig. 1). This will ensure that the outside edges of your quilt are on the straight of grain. The triangles will be sewn to your rows of quilt blocks before the rows are joined.

Fig. 1

Corner setting triangles

To make the 4 corner setting triangles, cut 2 squares in half once on the diagonal (fig. 2). The corner triangles will be sewn to the quilt top after your rows have been sewn together.

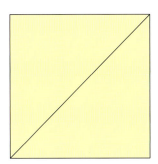

Fig. 2

When you add your triangles, they will be slightly larger than necessary. It is important to clean up the edges of your quilt top before you begin attaching your borders. Using a long ruler and your rotary cutter and mat, trim

the edges of the quilt top, leaving a ¼" seam allowance (fig. 3).

Fig. 3

Borders

Once your pieced quilt top is assembled and trimmed, you are ready to add your borders. Borders square up a quilt nicely and give it a more finished, almost framed appearance. Just as you might mat a quality photo or piece of artwork, many quilts are enhanced by the addition of one or more borders.

Many of the quilts in this book have two borders—a narrow inner border and a wider outer border. All the borders feature either corner blocks or long horizontal or vertical borders—no mitering involved, although you are welcome to do so if that is your preference.

Cutting and piecing border strips

The cutting charts tell you how many strips of fabric you will need to make your borders. If your quilt is wider than the length of your fabric strips, you will need to piece them to obtain enough length. To save fabric, I cut my strips across the 40" width of the fabric and piece them to make longer sections.

If you prefer not to piece your borders, buy a length of fabric several inches longer than the longest side of your quilt. Cut your strips along the length of the fabric. This generally takes more fabric than when the borders are pieced. You can use the extra fabric to make the binding for your quilt. When yardages for both methods are given, the non-pieced (greater) yardage is given in parentheses.

Setting Triangles and Borders

To piece two border strips together, lay them perpendicular to each other, right sides together. Mark a line from corner to corner as shown (fig. 4) and sew along that line.

Fig. 4

Trim the excess fabric, leaving a ¼" seam allowance (fig. 5).

Fig. 5

Press these seams open, unlike the seams within blocks that you press to one side. This creates a diagonal seam that lies flat, and is less obvious when the quilt is finished. An exception to making the diagonal seam involves a border with stripes that will run across the width of the border. In this case you will obtain nicer looking results by joining the strips end-to-end, so as not to break up the stripes.

Measuring borders

While you may know the size that your quilt should be, it is always a good idea to measure it before you cut your borders, as size variations do occur due to the slight, inevitable inconsistencies in seam allowances and trimming of blocks.

After cutting and piecing your border strips, measure them to the precise length that you need by simply placing the border strips across the body of your pressed quilt top—never along the edge, as it tends to stretch—and cutting to that length.

Cut the first pair of border strips for opposite sides of the quilt at the same time.

To attach the borders to your quilt, mark the center of the quilt top and the border strip. I like to do this by pressing a light crease with my iron, but a pin or chalk mark will work as well. Pin, matching the ends and centers, then pin at frequent intervals along the edge of the quilt. The borders may need to be eased just a bit to fit, but your quilt will square up nicely and look better if the borders are the same length.

Sew, using a ¼" seam allowance. Press the seam allowance toward the border.

After attaching the first two borders, repeat these steps for the remaining two borders.

Borders with corner blocks

When your borders include cornerstones, as do two of the quilts in this book, measure all four of your borders before sewing any of them to your quilt by laying them across the body of the quilt in pairs. Sew the first pair of borders to opposite sides of your quilt and press. Sew the corner blocks to each end of the second set of border strips. Then sew these borders to your quilt, matching the corner block seams to the first border seams. Press.

Stand back and admire the work you've just completed!

For detailed information on finishing your quilt, see the Three Bs: Backing, Batting, and Binding (pages 80–84).

The Quilts

The following quilts are all made using one or more of the four blocks presented in this book. The quilts are arranged according to the number of different blocks used in each quilt, beginning with the quilts that use just one block pattern and progressing to CABINS IN THE STARS—the only quilt that uses all four blocks.

It just amazed me as I designed these quilts, how changing one small aspect could affect the entire overall appearance. Color, scale, proportion, and the number of blocks all created significant differences in the way a quilt turned out. Please experiment with these patterns, using your own color schemes to make the quilts your own.

Refer back to the previous pages for assembly instructions for each type of block. Where there are variations in the methods of assembly, those instructions will be given as needed for the specific quilt.

One-Block Quilts:
Star Block

Twinkle, Twinkle
Made and quilted by the author, 43" x 43"
(See page 15 for an alternate size.)

Level of difficulty: Medium
Techniques: Partial seam; on-point construction
Finished block sizes: 6" x 6" and 12" x 12"

Twinkle, Twinkle

TWINKLE, TWINKLE is made by constructing the Star block in two sizes and arranging the blocks on point. I chose an assortment of pink fabrics for this quilt, but a Christmas or patriotic color scheme works equally well. For a fun variation just raid your stash of scraps and make each Star different.

If you are using an assortment of fabrics, keep in mind that you will need additional fabric for the background and setting triangles.

Making the Star Blocks

Construct the Star blocks according to the instructions on page 7. The unfinished blocks should measure 6½" x 6½" and 12½" x 12½".

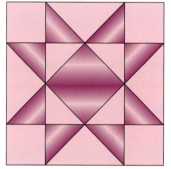

Make 9 small   Make 4 large

Materials for Twinkle, Twinkle

Finished quilt size: 43" x 43" (wall)

Assorted pink fabrics	1 yard (or ¼ yard of each color)
Background fabric	1⅝ yards
Narrow border	¼ yard
Wide border	⅝ yard
Binding	⅜ yard
Backing	2¼ yards
Batting	51" x 51"

Cutting Chart for Twinkle, Twinkle
Finished block sizes: 6" x 6" and 12" x 12" (wall)

Fabric	Piece code	# of strips	Strip width	Piece length	# of pieces
Assorted pinks	C-lg & B-sm	4	3½"	3½"	41
	C-sm	4	2"	2"	72
	B-lg	1	6½"	6½"	4
Background	C-lg	3	3½"	3½"	32
	C-sm	4	2"	2"	72
	D-lg	3	3½"	6½"	16
	D-sm	4	2"	3½"	36
	side setting triangles ⊠	1	10"	10"	3
	corner triangles ◩	1	7"	7"	2
Narrow border		4	1½"		
Wide border		5	4"		
Binding		5	2½"		
Batting		51" x 51"			
Backing		1 panel, 40" x 51" & 2 panels 10" x 25"			

Twinkle, Twinkle Assembly

1. Lay out all your blocks according to the diagram (fig. 1) before assembling them to be sure that the arrangement is to your liking.

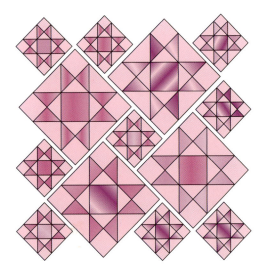

Fig. 1

2. Sew a side setting triangle to a small Star block, then sew this unit to a large Star block (fig. 2). Make 4 two-star units.

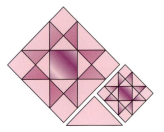

Fig. 2

3. Add a small Star block to one of the units with a partial seam as shown (fig. 3), matching the outer edges and sewing approximately two-thirds of the way across the small Star block. That is your partial seam. You'll come back to it later.

Stop sewing here

Fig. 3

4. Add the 3 remaining two-star units, going clockwise around the center block (fig. 4). Complete the partial seam as you finish joining the last two-star units.

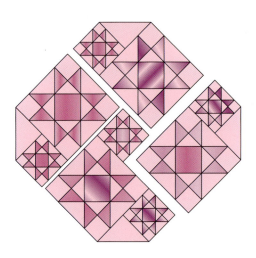

Fig. 4

5. Sew 2 side setting triangles to opposite sides of the remaining 4 small Star blocks (fig. 5).

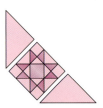

Fig. 5

6. Add these small Star corner units to the quilt top (fig. 6).

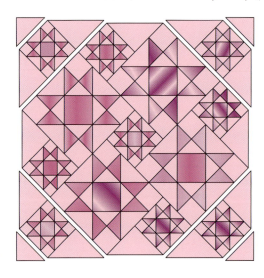

Fig. 6

Add the corner triangles as shown in figure 6. The triangles will be a bit too big, but just center them on the small Star blocks. Trim up the edges of your quilt, leaving a 1/4"–3/8" seam allowance beyond the points of the Star blocks.

Borders

Add the narrow inner border and the wider outer border, following the instructions on page 9.

Backing

Piece the backing panels according to the piecing diagram on page 80.

Materials for Twinkle, Twinkle

Finished quilt size: 55" x 55" (lap)

Red	1 yard
Green	¼ yard
Gold	¼ yard or 1 fat quarter
Cream background	2⅜ yards
Narrow border	⅜ yard
Wide border	⅞ yard
Binding	½ yard
Backing	3¾ yards
Batting	63" x 63"

Alternate Size and Colorway

Here is TWINKLE, TWINKLE in a different colorway and size. The unfinished blocks are 8½" x 8½" and 16½" x 16½". The finished quilt is 55" x 55". It is constructed exactly like the smaller quilt.

Cutting Chart for Twinkle, Twinkle

Finished block sizes: 8" x 8" and 16" x 16" (lap)

Fabric	Piece code	# of strips	Strip width	Piece length	# of pieces
Red	C-lg	4	4½"	4½"	32
	C-sm	5	2½"	2½"	72
Green	B-sm	1	4½"	4½"	9
Gold	B-lg	1	8½"	8½"	4
Cream background	C-lg	4	4½"	4½"	32
	C-sm	5	2½"	2½"	72
	D-lg	4	4½"	8½"	16
	D-sm	4	2½"	4½"	36
	side setting triangles ⊠	1	12¾"	12¾"	3
	corner triangles ◺	1	9"	9"	2
Narrow border		6	1½"		
Wide border		6	4½"		
Binding		6	2½"		
Batting		63" x 63"			
Backing		2 panels, 40" x 63"			

One-Block Quilts: Star Block

Galaxy
Made and quilted by the author, 74" x 74"

Level of difficulty: Medium
Finished block sizes: 8" x 8"

Patchwork 4 Ways *by Kathleen Hulett*

Galaxy

This is a scrap and fat-quarter-friendly quilt with 32 fat quarters making 64 Star blocks in a variety of colors. Each Star block utilizes three different fabrics and each fabric shows up in six different blocks. If you want to make a smaller quilt, you will need half as many fat quarters as the number of blocks desired. So, if you have 10 fat quarters, you can make 20 blocks. Don't you just love it when the math is that easy?

How much fabric do I need?

32 fat quarters
Narrow border: ½ yard
Wide border: 1⅛ yards (2¼ yards if you don't want to piece your border)
Binding: ⅔ yard (omit if you are binding with the same fabric as your wide border and buy the 2¼ yards border fabric)
Backing: 4⅔ yards (assumes at least 42" fabric width)
Batting: 82" x 82"

What do I need to cut?

From each fat quarter:
Cut: five 2½" x 22" strips into:
      thirty-two 2½" C squares
      four 2½" x 4½" D rectangles

Cut: one 4½" x 22" strip into:
      four 2½" x 4½" D rectangles
      two 4½" B squares

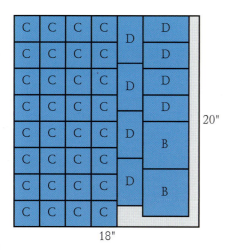

Fig. 1

This yields the pieces for two complete Star blocks, but all in one fabric. Not terribly exciting, I will admit. Just mix and match pieces from different fat quarters to obtain a variety of colors for each block.

	# of strips	Strip width
Narrow border	8	1½"
Wide border	8	4½"
Binding	8	2½"
Batting	82" x 82"	
Backing	2 panels 40" x 82"	

How many blocks do I need to make?

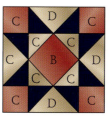

Fig. 2   Make 64

Making the Star Blocks

Referring to figure 2, construct 64 Star blocks according to the instructions on page 7, using three colors for each Star as follows:

Color 1: one square B and four C squares for the center and corner patches
Color 2: four C squares for the center and four D rectangles for the Flying Geese units
Color 3: eight C squares for the Flying Geese star points

Arrange the blocks in an 8 x 8 layout. Join the blocks into rows (fig. 3) and join the rows.

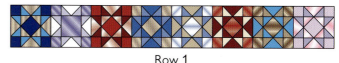

Row 1

Fig. 3

Borders

Add the narrow inner border and the wide outer border, following the instructions on page 9.

Backing

Piece the backing panels according to the piecing diagram on page 80.

One-Block Quilts:
Log Cabin Block

Who Let the Dogs Out?

Made by Linda Mosley of Columbia, Missouri
Quilted by the author, 46" x 58"
(See pages 20–21 for alternate sizes.)
Level of difficulty: Easy
Finished block size: 6" x 6"

Who Let the Dogs Out?

When I looked at this quilt, I thought it resembled a chain-link fence. When I found the border fabric with the dog print, I just knew what the name of this quilt had to be. You can really have some fun with the fabrics making this one. I know that I did!

How much fabric do I need?

Materials for Who Let the Dogs Out?	
Finished quilt size: 46" x 58" (lap)	
12 colors	¼ yard
White	½ yard
Dark blue	½ yard
Narrow border & binding	⅞ yard
Wide border print	1 yard (1⅝*)
Backing	3¼ yards
Batting	54" x 66"

* Amount needed if you don't want to piece your border.

How many blocks do I need to make?

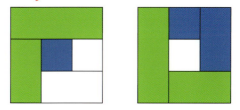

Make 2 of each of 12 colors.

Making the Log Cabin Blocks

1. Construct 48 Log Cabin blocks according to the instructions on page 8. The unfinished blocks should measure 6½" x 6½".

2. Make 12 four-block units, each of 4 same-color blocks, orienting them as shown (fig. 1). Alternate the direction that you press the seams to minimize bulk. If you press all of your units so that the seams go toward the single long strip of each unit, you'll be in good shape.

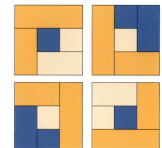

Fig. 1

What do I need to cut?

Cutting Chart for Who Let the Dogs Out?				Finished block size: 6" x 6" (lap)	
Fabric	Piece code	# of strips	Strip width	Piece length	# of pieces
Each of 12 colors	E	1	2½"	4½"	4
	D	1	2½"	6½"	4
Dark blue	B	3	2½"	2½"	48
	E	3	2½"	4½"	24
White	B	3	2½"	2½"	48
	E	3	2½"	4½"	24
Narrow border		6	1½"		
Wide border		6	4½"		
Binding		6	2½"		
Batting		54" x 66"			
Backing		2 panels, 40" x 54"			

Who Let the Dogs Out? Assembly

1. Lay out the four-block units in a 3 x 4 arrangement.

2. Sew the blocks into rows. Press, alternating the direction of the seams as before (fig. 2).

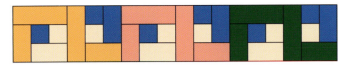

Fig. 2

Alternate Sizes and Colorways

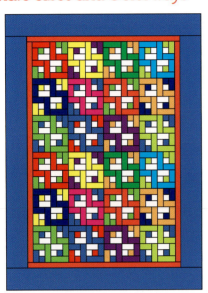

3. Sew the completed rows together.

Borders

4. Add the narrow inner border and the wide outer border, following the instructions on page 9.

Backing

Piece the backing panels according to the piecing diagram on page 80.

Materials for Who Let the Dogs Out?

Finished quilt size: 75" x 105" (twin)

12 colors	⅜ yard
White	1⅜ yards
Dark blue	1⅜ yards
Narrow border & binding	⅝ yard
Wide border print	1¾ yards (2¾*)
Backing	6⅝ yards, 42" width
Batting	83" x 113"

* Amount needed if you don't want to piece your border.

Cutting Chart for Who Let the Dogs Out?   Finished block size: 7½" x 7½" (twin)

Fabric	Piece code	# of strips	Strip width	Piece length	# of pieces
Each of	E	2	3"	5½"	8
12 colors	D	2	3"	8"	8
Dark blue	B	8	3"	3"	96
	E	7	3"	5½"	48
White	B	8	3"	3"	96
	E	7	3"	5½"	48
Narrow border		9	2"		
Wide border		9	6½"		
Binding		10	2½"		
Batting		83" x 113"			
Backing		2 panels, 42" x 113"			

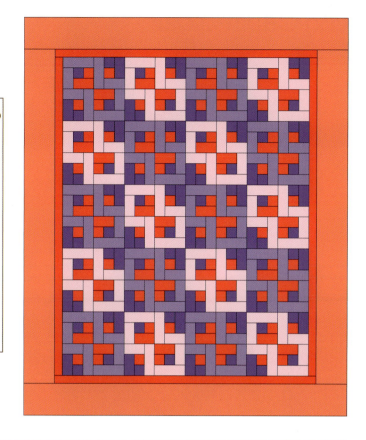

Materials for Who Let the Dogs Out?

Finished quilt size: 87" x 105" (queen)

Pink & light blue	1¾ yards each
Red & medium blue	1⅝ yards each
Narrow border & binding	1¼ yards
Wide border print	2 yards (2¾*)
Backing	8½ yards
Batting	95" x 113"

* Amount needed if you don't want to piece your border.

Cutting Chart for Who Let the Dogs Out?

Finished block size: 9" x 9" (queen)

Fabric	Piece code	# of strips	Strip width	Piece length	# of pieces
Pink	E	7	3½"	6½"	40
	D	10	3½"	9½"	40
Light blue	E	7	3½"	6½"	40
	D	10	3½"	9½"	40
Red	B	8	3½"	3½"	80
	E	7	3½"	6½"	40
Medium blue	B	8	3½"	3½"	80
	E	7	3½"	6½"	40
Narrow border		9	2"		
Wide border		10	6½"		
Binding		10	2½"		
Batting		95" x 113"			
Backing		3 panels, 40" x 95"			

One-Block Quilts:
Log Cabin Block

Building Blocks
Made by the author, 44" x 44"
(See page 25 for an alternate size.)

Level of difficulty: Medium
Techniques: Partial seam; on-point construction
Finished block sizes: 6" x 6" and 12" x 12"

Building Blocks

I made BUILDING BLOCKS as a Christmas quilt, but by changing the colors to pastels or bright colors, it makes a wonderful baby or child's quilt.

This quilt may look complicated, but it's really made from just one block—the Log Cabin—in two sizes. The arrangement of the blocks is exactly the same as in TWINKLE, TWINKLE. Check it out! The method of joining the blocks, initially using a partial seam, is the same as well.

How much fabric do I need?

Materials for Building Blocks

Finished quilt size: 44" x 44" (wall)	
Center color	¼ yard
5 colors	¼ yard each
Neutral (setting triangles)	⅝ yard
Narrow border & binding	⅝ yard
Wide border	⅝ yard (1⅜*)
Backing	2⅛ yards
Batting	52" x 52"

* Amount needed if you don't want to piece your border.

What do I need to cut?

Cutting Chart for Building Blocks
Finished block size: 6" x 6" and 12" x 12" (wall)

Fabric	Piece code	# of strips	Strip width	Piece length	# of pieces
Block centers	C – lg	1	4½"	4½"	4
	C – sm	1	2½"	2½"	9
4 other colors	C, D, E	1	4½"	4½"	1
				8½"	2
				12½"	1
		1	2½"	2½"	2*
				4½"	4*
				6½"	2*

* cut one more piece from each color to make 1 more small block

Fabric	Piece code	# of strips	Strip width	Piece length	# of pieces
Side setting triangles ⊠		1	10"	10"	3
Corner triangles ◸		1	7"	7"	2
Narrow border		4	1½"		
Wide border		4	4½"		
Border cornerstones (cut from one of the block fabrics)		1	4½"	4½"	4
Binding		5	2½"		
Batting			52" x 52"		
Backing			1 panel, 40" x 52" & 2 panels, 10" x 26"		

How many blocks do I need to make?

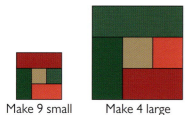

Make 9 small   Make 4 large

Making the Blocks

Make 9 small and 4 large Log Cabin blocks according to the instructions on page 8.

Building Blocks Assembly

1. Lay out all your blocks according to the diagram (fig. 1) before assembling them to be sure that the arrangement is to your liking. The individual blocks can be turned in any direction you like, but the arrangement of the blocks must be as shown.

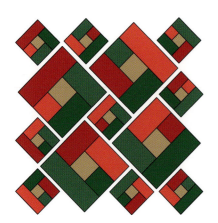

Fig. 1

2. Sew a side setting triangle to a small Log Cabin block, then sew this unit to a large Log Cabin block (fig. 2). Make 4 units like this.

Fig. 2   Make 4

3. Add a small Log Cabin block to one of the units with a partial seam as shown (fig. 3), matching the outer edges and sewing approximately two-thirds of the way across the small Log Cabin block. That is your partial seam. You'll come back to it later.

Fig. 3

4. Add the 3 remaining units, going clockwise around the center block (fig. 4). Complete the partial seam as you finish joining the last unit.

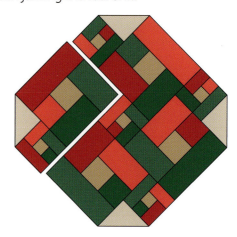

Fig. 4

5. Sew 2 side setting triangles to opposite sides of the remaining 4 small Log Cabin blocks (fig. 5).

Fig. 5   Make 4

6. Sew these units to the long edges of the quilt top and sew the remaining 4 small triangles to the corners of your quilt top (fig. 6). The triangles will be a bit too big, but just center them on the small Log Cagin blocks.

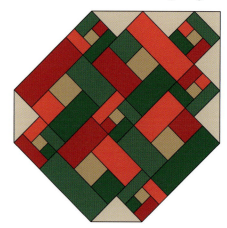

Fig. 6

Trim up the edges of your quilt, leaving a ¼" seam allowance beyond the corners of the Log Cabin blocks.

Borders

Add the narrow inner border and the wide outer border, following the instructions on page 9.

Backing

Piece the backing panels according to the piecing diagram on page 80.

Alternate Size and Colorway

Materials for Building Blocks

Finished quilt size: 52" x 52" (lap)

Center color	⅓ yard
5 colors	⅝ yard each
Setting triangles	⅝ yard
Narrow border & binding	¾ yard
Wide border	⅞ yard (1½*)
Backing	3½ yards
Batting	60" x 60"

* Amount needed if you don't want to piece your border.

BUILDING BLOCKS in green and lavender colorway, made by Marjorie Hulett of Garnett, Kansas, and quilted by the author, 52" x 52"

The unfinished blocks will measure 8" x 8" and 15½"x 15½".

Cutting Chart for Building Blocks

Finished block sizes: 7½" x 7½" and 15" x 15" (lap)

Fabric	Piece code	# of strips	Strip width	Piece length	# of pieces
Block centers	C – lg	1	5½"	5½"	4
	C – sm	1	3"	3"	9
4 other colors	C, D, E	2	5½"	5½"	1
				10½"	2
				15½"	1
		2	3"	3"	2*
				5½"	4*
				8½"	2*

*Cut one more piece from each color to make 1 more small block.

Fabric		# of strips	Strip width	Piece length	# of pieces
Side setting triangles ⊠		1	11⅜"	11⅜"	3
Corner triangles ◹		1	8"	8"	2
Narrow border		5	1½"		
Wide border		6	4½"		
Border cornerstones (cut from one of the block fabrics)		1	4½"	4½"	4
Binding		6	2½"		
Batting			60" x 60"		
Backing			2 panels, 40" x 60"		

One-Block Quilts: Stripe Block

Basket Weave

Made and quilted by the author, 58" x 70"
(See pages 28–29 for alternate sizes.)

Level of difficulty: Easy
Finished block size: 6" x 6"

Patchwork 4 Ways *by Kathleen Hulett*

Basket Weave

This quilt is made from just one block, using different colors for the outer stripes of the vertical and horizontal blocks.

How much fabric do I need?

Materials for	Basket Weave
Finished quilt size: 58" x 70" (lap)	
Centers	1½ yards
Outside stripe	⅞ yard
Outer stripe 2	⅞ yard
Narrow border	⅜ yard
Wide border	1⅛ yards (1⅞*)
Binding	⅝ yard
Backing	4½ yards
Batting	66" x 78"

* Amount needed if you don't want to piece your border.

How many blocks do I need to make?

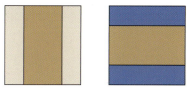

Make 40 of each

Making the Stripe Blocks

1. Make 14 strip-sets, all with the same center fabric, but half with one color outer strips and half with a second color outer strips. Follow the instructions on page 8.

2. Cut 80 segments 6½" wide from the strip-sets.

Basket Weave Assembly

1. Lay out your blocks in an 8 x 10 arrangement as shown (fig. 1), alternating the direction and color of the stripes.

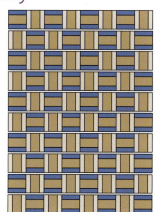

Fig. 1

What do I need to cut?

Cutting Chart for	Basket Weave	Finished block size: 6" x 6" (lap)			

Fabric	Piece code	# of strips	Strip width	Piece length	# of pieces
Centers	W	14*	3½"	6½"	80
Horizontal stripes	N	14*	2"	6½"	80
Vertical stripes	N	14*	2"	6½"	80
Narrow border		6	1½"		
Wide border		8	4½"		
Binding		8	2½"		
Batting		66" x 78"			
Backing		2 panels, 40" x 78"			

* Strip piece before cutting to length

2. Sew the blocks into rows, pressing the seams in opposite directions. Then join the rows.

Borders

Add the narrow inner border and the wide outer border, following the instructions on page 9.

Backing

Piece the backing panels according to the piecing diagram on page 80.

Alternate Sizes and Colorways

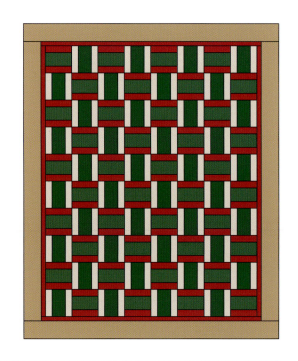

Materials for Basket Weave

Finished quilt size: 58" x 82" (twin)

Centers	1¾ yards
Outside stripe	1 yard
Outer stripe 2	1 yard
Narrow border	⅜ yard
Wide border	1⅛ yards (2¼*)
Binding	⅝ yard
Backing	5⅜ yards
Batting	66" x 90"

* Amount needed if you don't want to piece your border.

Cutting Chart for Basket Weave

Finished block size: 6" x 6" (twin)

Fabric	Piece code	# of strips	Strip width	Piece length	# of pieces
Centers	W	16*	3½"	6½"	96
Horizontal stripes	N	16*	2"	6½"	96
Vertical stripes	N	16*	2"	6½"	96
Narrow border		8	1½"		
Wide border		8	4½"		
Binding		8	2½"		
Batting		66" x 90"			
Backing		2 panels, 40" x 90"			

* Strip piece before cutting to length.

Materials for Basket Weave

Finished quilt size: 82" x 90" (queen)

Centers	3⅛ yards
Outside stripe	1¾ yards
Outer stripe 2	1¾ yards
Narrow border	1¾ yards
Wide border	1⅜ yards (2⅝*)
Binding	¾ yard
Backing	7⅞ yards
Batting	90" x 98"

* Amount needed if you don't want to piece your border.

Cutting Chart for Basket Weave

Finished block size: 8" x 8" (queen)

Fabric	Piece code	# of strips	Strip width	Piece length	# of pieces
Centers	W	23*	4½"	8½"	90
Horizontal stripes	N	23*	2½"	8½"	90
Vertical stripes	N	23*	2½"	8½"	90
Narrow border		8	1½"		
Wide border		10	4½"		
Binding		10	2½"		
Batting		90" x 98"			
Backing		3 panels, 40" x 90"			

* Strip piece before cutting to length.

One-Block Quilts:
Stripe Block

Little Lamb
Made and quilted by the author, 42" x 42"

Level of difficulty: Easy
Technique: On-point construction
Finished block size: 6" x 6"

Little Lamb

This quilt is made with 25 Stripe blocks, using three coordinating colors. The blocks are then set on point to make a simple, but delightful baby quilt.

Refer to the section on side setting and corner triangles (page 9) for instructions on cutting them for this quilt.

How much fabric do I need?

Materials for Little Lamb	
Finished quilt size: 42" x 42" (baby)	
Light pink stripe	½ yard
Dark pink stripe	½ yard
Yellow stripe	½ yard
Side setting triangles	⅜ yard
Narrow border	¼ yard
Wide border	½ yard
Binding	½ yard
Backing	1¾ yards
Batting	46" x 46"

How many blocks do I need to make?

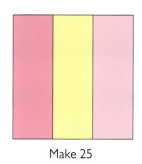

Make 25

Making the Blocks

1. Strip piece the Stripe blocks using all three colors of fabric in each strip-set, according to the instructions on page 8.

2. Cut twenty-five 6½" segments from the strip-sets. The unfinished blocks should measure 6½" x 6½".

What do I need to cut?

Cutting Chart for Little Lamb — Finished block size: 6" x 6" (baby)

Fabric	Piece code	# of strips	Strip width	Piece length	# of pieces
Light pink*	N-1	5	2½"	6½"	25
Dark pink*	N-2	5	2½"	6½"	25
Yellow*	W	5	2½"	6½"	25
Side setting triangles ⊠		1	8½"	8½"	3
Corner triangles ◹		1	4½"	4½"	2
Narrow border		4	1½"		
Wide border		4	3½"		
Binding		5	2½"		
Batting		46" x 46"			
Backing		1 panel, 40" x 46" & 2 panels, 7" x 23"			

*Strip piece before cutting to length.

Little Lamb Assembly

1. Lay out the blocks and setting triangles in diagonal rows as shown.

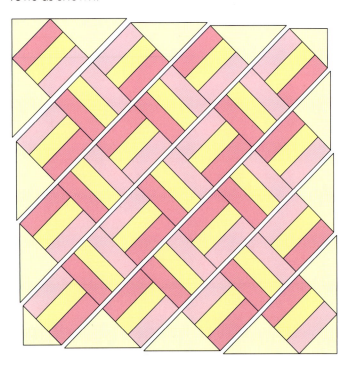

2. Join the blocks and setting triangles into rows. Press the seams toward the single strip in the neighboring blocks.

3. Sew the rows together, matching and pinning seams carefully.

4. Add the corner setting triangles as shown above. The triangles will be a bit too big, but just center them on the corner Stripe blocks. Trim up the edges of your quilt, leaving a ¼"–⅜" seam allowance beyond the corners of the Stripe blocks.

Borders

Add the narrow inner border and the wide outer border, following the instructions on page 9.

Backing

Piece the backing panels according to the piecing diagram on page 80.

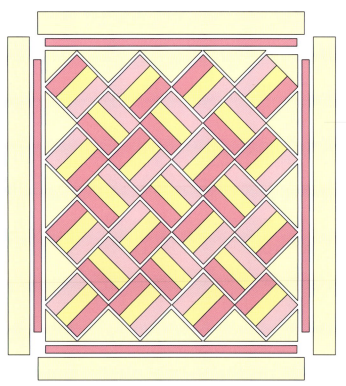

Snow Goose Gaggle
Made and quilted by the author, 58" x 74"

Level of difficulty: Easy
Technique: Piano Key border
Finished block size: 6" x 8"

Snow Goose Gaggle

This gaggle of Snow Goose blocks gives you a chance to use up some scraps while making a fun quilt. I made this one for my youngest grandson.

How much fabric do I need?

Materials for Gaggle

Finished quilt size: 58" x 74" (lap)	
Background	3⅛ yards
Assorted colorful fabrics for blocks & Piano Key border	3½ yards total
Narrow border	⅜ yard
Binding	⅝ yard
Backing	4 yards, 42" width
Batting	66" x 82"

How many blocks do I need to make?

Make 64

Making the Snow Goose Blocks

Construct the Snow Goose blocks according to the instructions on page 8. The unfinished blocks should measure 6½" x 8½".

Snow Goose Gaggle Assembly

1. Lay out your blocks in an 8 x 8 arrangement. Notice that every other block is oriented in the opposite direction (fig. 1, page 35). This arrangement results in large open spaces between the colorful triangles, giving you space for quilting a design of your choice. In the quilt shown, I used a spiral star motif, but have also used a turtle in that space on another similar quilt. If you like appliqué, those spaces would lend themselves well to colorful appliqué motifs.

What do I need to cut?

Cutting Chart for Gaggle   Finished block size: 6" x 8" (lap)

Fabric	Piece code	# of strips	Strip width	Piece length	# of pieces
Background	A	16	6½"	8½"	64
Geese "wings"	B	16	4½"	4½"	128
Border cornerstones		1	4½"	4½"	4
Narrow border		7	1½"		
Wide border		See instructions for Piano Key Border, page 35.			
Binding		8	2½"		
Batting		66" x 82"			
Backing		2 panels, 42" x 66"			

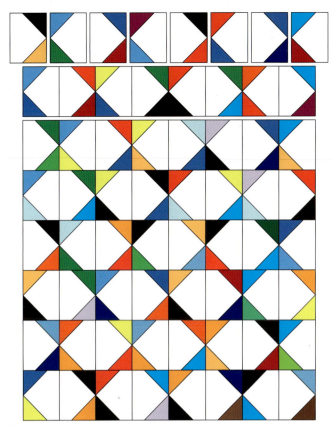

Fig. 1

2. When you have your blocks laid out to your liking, sew the blocks into rows, then sew the rows together.

> *Tip: To keep track of which block goes where in each row, number each block with a small piece of paper pinned to each block. It may be time consuming, but is well worth the effort when you need to know which block comes next in the row. It also saves a lot of hopping back and forth from your machine to wherever you have your blocks laid out, as you can then pick up all of the blocks for any given row at one time and know where to put them.

3. When your rows are all sewn together, trim up the edges of your quilt with your long ruler and rotary cutter.

Borders

1. Add the narrow inner border following the instructions on page 9.

2. Dig into your scrap bag again to make the scrappy Piano Key border. You will need an assortment of fabric strips approximately 2"–3" wide. They do not have to be all the same width.

3. Make a strip-set of a variety of strips of similar length. Cut into 4½" segments (fig. 2).

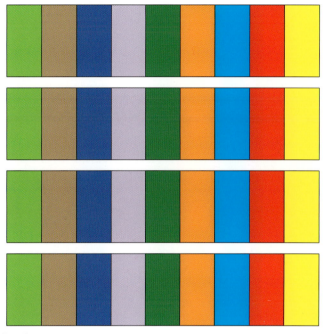

Fig. 2

4. Sew segments end-to-end for the length you need for your quilt borders (fig. 3). Measure your completed rows of border segments as you would any other border and sew them to your quilt top.

Fig. 3

Backing

Piece the backing panels according to the piecing diagram on page 80.

One-Block Quilts:
Snow Goose Block

Fly Away Home
Made and quilted by the author, 33" x 42"
(See pages 38–39 for alternate sizes.)

Level of difficulty: Medium
Technique: Partial assembly of blocks
Finished block size 3" x 4"

Fly Away Home

Whether you see geese, butterflies, or patriotic stars, this small quilt makes up quickly into a nice wallhanging. It is made with just the Snow Goose block, although some of the geese have only one "wing." Be careful as you construct the blocks to ensure that the wings are in the right place for each block. This one is a bit trickier than it looks, but well worth the effort.

How much fabric do I need?

Materials for Fly Away Home

Finished quilt size: 33" x 42" (wall)

Tan	1 yard
Red	⅜ yard
Dark blue	⅛ yard
White	¼ yard
Narrow border	included in Red yardage
Wide border	⅜ yard
Binding	⅜ yard
Backing	1⅜ yards
Batting	37" x 46"

How many blocks do I need to make?

wall / twin quilt

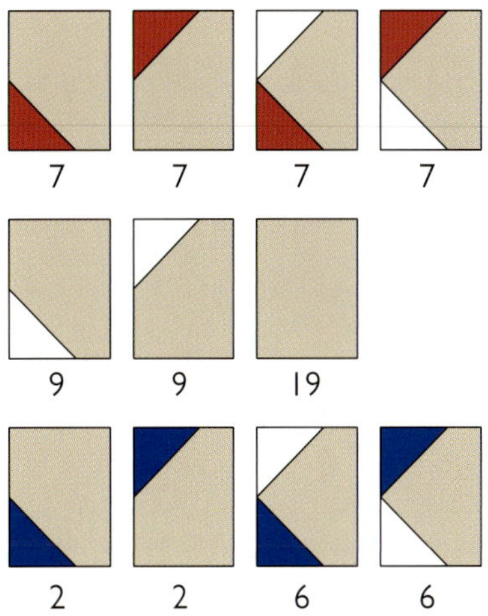

7	7	7	7
9	9	19	
2	2	6	6

Making the Snow Goose Blocks

Construct your Snow Goose blocks according to the instructions on page 8. Note that some of the geese have only one wing. Be careful or your wings are liable to end up on the wrong side of the goose!

Fly Away Home Assembly

1. Arrange the blocks according to the assembly diagram on page 38.

What do I need to cut?

Cutting Chart for Fly Away Home

Finished block size: 3" x 4" (wall)

Fabric	Piece code	# of strips	Strip width	Piece length	# of pieces
Red	B	2	2½"	2½"	28
Dark blue	B	1	2½"	2½"	16
White	B	3	2½"	2½"	44
Tan	A	9	3½"	4½"	81
Narrow border		4	1⅛"		
Wide border		4	3"		
Binding		4	2½"		
Batting			37" x 46"		
Backing			1 panel, 40" x 46"		

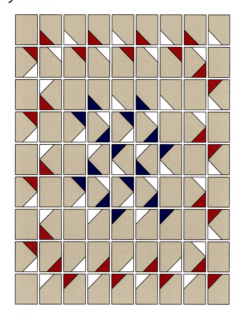

Alternate Sizes and Colorway

A twin size quilt is made exactly like the wall/crib size simply by making larger blocks that finish to 6" x 8" in a 9 x 9 block setting as shown.

A queen size quilt is made with 6" x 8" blocks in a 13 x 13 block setting.

2. Sew the blocks into rows, then join the rows. Each row is different, so pay careful attention when you sew your blocks together.

Borders

Add the narrow inner border and the wide outer border following the instructions on page 9.

Backing

Piece the backing panels according to the piecing diagram on page 80.

Materials for Fly Away Home

Finished quilt size: 64" x 82" (twin)

Tan or light blue	3½ yards
Red	⅝ yard
Dark blue	⅜ yard
White	⅞ yard
Narrow border	⅜ yard
Wide border	1⅛ yards
Binding	⅔ yard
Backing	5¼ yards
Batting	72" x 90"

Cutting Chart for Fly Away Home
Finished block size: 6" x 8" (twin)

Fabric	Piece code	# of strips	Strip width	Piece length	# of pieces
Red	B	4	4½"	4½"	28
Dark blue	B	2	4½"	4½"	16
White	B	6	4½"	4½"	44
Tan or light blue	A	14	8½"	6½"	81
Narrow border		8	1½"		
Wide border		8	4½"		
Binding		8	2½"		
Batting			72" x 90"		
Backing			2 panels, 40" x 90"		

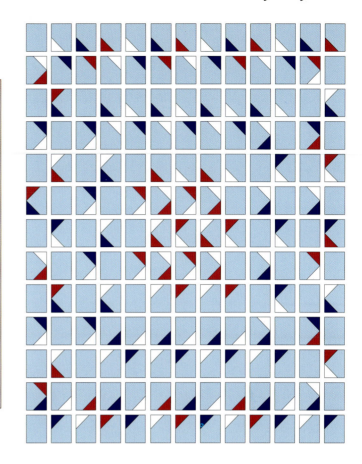

Materials for Fly Away Home

Finished quilt size: 94" x 120" (queen)

Tan or light blue	7¼ yards
Red	⅞ yard
Dark blue	1⅛ yards
White	1⅜ yards
Narrow border	¾ yard
Wide border	2⅓ yards
Binding	1 yard
Backing	11¼ yards
Batting	102" x 128"

Cutting Chart for Fly Away Home

Finished block size: 6" x 8" (queen)

Fabric	Piece code	# of strips	Strip width	Piece length	# of pieces
Red	B	6	4½"	4½"	44
Dark blue	B	8	4½"	4½"	58
White	B	10	4½"	4½"	74
Tan or light blue	A	29	8½"	6½"	169
Narrow border		10	2½"		
Wide border		12	6½"		
Binding		12	2½"		
Batting		102" x 128"			
Backing		3 panels, 40" x 128"			

Two-Block Quilts

Baby Blue Stars & Stripes
Made and quilted by the author, 44" x 44"
(See pages 42–43 for an alternate size.)

Level of difficulty: Easy–medium
Technique: Sashing strips
Finished block size: 6" x 6"

Baby Blue Stars & Stripes

Baby Blue Stars & Stripes is a two-block quilt with sashing between the blocks. You can easily adapt this pattern to any size quilt by changing the number of blocks that you make.

How much fabric do I need?

Materials for Baby Blue Stars & Stripes	
Finished quilt size: 44" x 44" (crib)	
Dark blue	¾ yard
Light blue	⅜ yard
Yellow	⅞ yard
Sashing	½ yard
Sashing cornerstones	⅛ yard
Border	¾ yard (1⅜*)
Binding	⅜ yard
Backing	2 yards
Batting	48" x 48"

* Amount needed if you don't want to piece your border.

How many blocks do I need to make?

Make 12   Make 13

Making the Star and Stripe Blocks

1. Construct 12 Star blocks according to the instructions on page 7.

2. Construct 13 Stripe blocks according to the instructions on page 8.

3. Sew 2 sashing strips to opposite sides of 8 Star blocks. Sew 1 sashing strip to 4 Star blocks as shown (fig. 1).

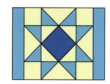

Fig. 1

What do I need to cut?

Cutting Chart for Baby Blue Stars & Stripes					Finished block size: 6" x 6" (crib)
Fabric	**Piece code**	**# of strips**	**Strip width**	**Piece length**	**# of pieces**
Dark blue	N	6*	2½"	6½"	26
	B	2	3½"	3½"	12
Light blue	C	5	2"	2"	96
Yellow	C	5	2"	2"	96
	D	3	3½"	2"	48
	W	3*	2½"	6½"	13
Sashing		10	1½"	6½"	60
Sashing cornerstones		2	1½"	1½"	36
Border		5	4½"		
Binding		5	2½"		
Batting		48" x 48"			
Backing		1 panel, 40" x 48" & 2 panels, 10" x 24"			

* Strip piece before cutting to length

Baby Blue Stars & Stripes Assembly

1. Assemble rows of blocks and rows of sashing strips and cornerstones as shown (fig. 2). Press the seam allowances toward the sashing strips.

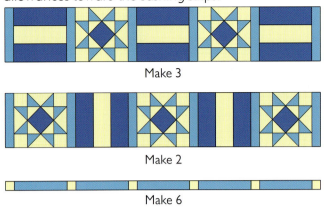

Make 3

Make 2

Make 6

Fig. 2

2. Join the rows, carefully matching and pinning the seams. Note that the sashing also serves as a narrow inner border (fig. 3).

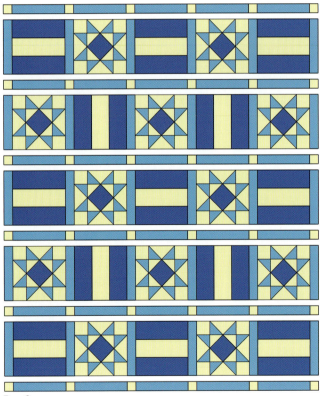

Fig. 3

3. Clean up the edges of your quilt top using your long ruler and rotary cutter, and you're ready to add your borders.

Borders

Add the wide outer border following the instructions on page 9.

Backing

Piece the backing panels according to the piecing diagram on page 80.

Alternate Size and Colorway

PATRIOTIC STARS & STRIPES presents a different colorway and size. The finished blocks are 6" x 6" and the finished quilt is 58" x 58". It is constructed in the same way as the smaller quilt.

Materials for	Patriotic Stars & Stripes
Finished quilt size: 58" x 58" (lap)	
Red	1 yard
Blue	⅝ yard
White	1½ yards
Sashing	⅞ yard
Sashing cornerstones	¼ yard
Border	⅞ yard (1¾*)
Binding	⅝ yard
Backing	3⅞ yards
Batting	66" x 66"

* Amount needed if you don't want to piece your border.

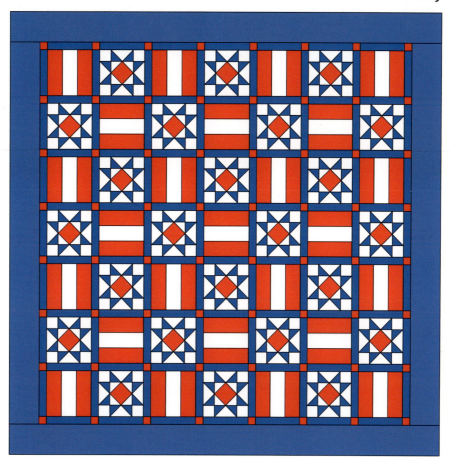

Cutting Chart for Patriotic Stars & Stripes

Finished block size: 6" x 6" (lap)

Fabric	Piece code	# of strips	Strip width	Piece length	# of pieces
Red	N	8*	2½"	6½"	50
	B	3	3½"	3½"	24
Blue	C	10	2"	2"	192
White	C	10	2"	2"	192
	D	5	3½"	2"	96
	W	4*	2½"	6½"	25
Sashing – blue		19	1½"	6½"	112
Cornerstones – red		3	1½"	1½"	64
Wide border		6	4½"		
Binding		7	2½"		
Batting		66" x 66"			
Backing		2 panels, 40" x 66"			

* Strip piece before cutting to length.

Cactus Flowers

Made and quilted by the author, 44" x 44"

Level of difficulty: Medium
Techniques: On-point construction
Finished block size: 8" x 8"

Cactus Flowers

CACTUS FLOWERS uses the same two blocks as the STARS & STRIPES quilts, but sets them on point for an different look.

How much fabric do I need?

Materials for Cactus Flowers	
Finished quilt size: 44" x 44" (lap)	
Cream	1⅝ yards
Teal	½ yard
Peach	½ yard
Narrow border	¼ yard
Wide border	¾ yard (1⅜*)
Binding	½ yard
Backing	2 yards
Batting	48" x 48"

* Amount needed if you don't want to piece your border.

How many blocks do I need to make?

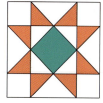

Make 9

Make 4

Making the Star and Stripe Blocks

1. Construct 9 Star blocks according to the instructions on page 7.

2. Construct 4 Stripe blocks according to the instructions on page 8.

What do I need to cut?

Cutting Chart for Cactus Flowers — Finished block size: 8" x 8" (lap)

Fabric	Piece code	# of strips	Strip width	Piece length	# of pieces
Teal	B	2	4½"	4½"	9
	N*	2	2½"	8½"	8
Peach	C	5	2½"	2½"	72
Cream	C	5	2½"	2½"	72
	D	5	2½"	4½"	36
	W*	1	4½"	8½"	4
Side setting triangles ⊠		1	12"	12"	2
Corner triangles ◺		1	6"	6"	2
Narrow border		4	1½"		
Wide border		5	4½"		
Binding		5	2½"		
Batting		48" x 48"			
Backing		1 panel, 40" x 48" & 2 panels, 10" x 24"			

* Strip piece before cutting to length.

Cactus Flowers

Cactus Flowers Assembly

1. Lay out the blocks and the side and corner setting triangles in diagonal rows as shown.

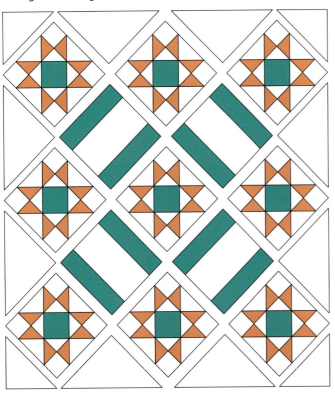

2. Join the blocks into rows, pressing the seams in each row in opposite directions. Join the rows, carefully matching and pinning the seams. Press all the seams in the same direction.

3. Trim up the edges of your quilt with your long ruler and rotary cutter, leaving a ¼"–⅜" seam allowance beyond the points of your blocks.

Borders

Add the narrow inner border and the wide outer border, following the instructions on page 9.

Backing

Piece the backing panels according to the piecing diagram on page 80.

Driftwood

Made and quilted by the author, 52" x 64"
(See pages 49–50 for alternate sizes.)

Level of difficulty: Easy
Finished block size: 6" x 6"

Driftwood

I've always been fascinated by the ocean and by the driftwood that washes up on to the shore. The wavy pattern created by the arrangement of the Log Cabin and Stripe blocks reminds me of just that.

How much fabric do I need?

Materials for Driftwood	
Finished quilt size: 52" x 64" (lap)	
Wavy stripe (outer stripes & center square)	1 yard
Yellow (center stripe & small edges of log cabins)	1 yard
Purple (long edges of log cabins)	⅞ yard
Narrow border	⅜ yard
Wide border	1 yard (1⅔*)
Binding	⅝ yard
Backing	3½ yards
Batting	60" x 72"

* Amount needed if you don't want to piece your border. If you want to bind your quilt with the same fabric, you can omit the binding yardage when you buy this quantity for your wide border.

How many blocks do I need to make?

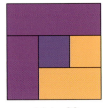
Make 32

Make 31

Making the Log Cabin and Stripe Blocks

1. Construct 32 Log Cabin blocks according to the instructions on page 8.

2. Construct 31 Stripe blocks according to the instructions on page 8. The strips in the Stripe block are all the same width, instead of one wide and two narrow strips.

Driftwood Assembly

1. Arrange the blocks in rows as shown on page 49.

What do I need to cut?

Cutting Chart for Driftwood — Finished block size: 6" x 6" (lap)

Fabric	Piece code	# of strips	Strip width	Piece length	# of pieces
Wavy stripe	N	12*	2½"	6½"	62*
	C	2	2½"	2½"	32
Yellow	W	6*	2½"	6½"	31*
	C	2	2½"	2½"	32
	D	4	2½"	4½"	32
Purple	D	4	2½"	4½"	32
	E	6	2½"	6½"	32
Narrow border		6	1½"		
Wide border		7	4½"		
Binding		7	2½"		
Batting		60" x 72"			
Backing		2 panels, 40" x 60"			

* Strip piece before cutting to length

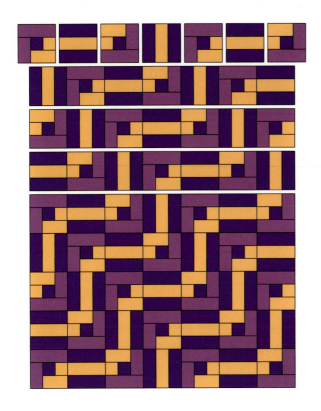

3. Clean up the edges of your quilt top using your long ruler and rotary cutter, and you're ready to add your borders.

Borders

Add the narrow inner border and the wide outer border following the instructions on page 9.

Backing

Piece the backing panels according to the piecing diagram on page 80.

Alternate Sizes

The twin size quilt is made with 9 rows of six 9" x 9"(finished) blocks each.

The queen size quilt is made with 12 rows of ten 7½"x 7½" (finished) blocks each.

Both sizes are constructed in the same manner as the lap size quilt.

2. Join the blocks into rows, pressing the seams in each row in opposite directions. Join the rows, carefully matching and pinning the seams. Press all the seams in the same direction.

Materials for Driftwood	
Finished quilt size: 64" x 91" (twin)	
Color 1 (outer stripes & center square)	1⅞ yards
Color 2 (center stripe & small edges of Log Cabins)	1⅝ yards
Color 3 (long edges of Log Cabins)	1⅓ yards
Narrow border	½ yard
Wide border	1¼ yards (2⅝*)
Binding	¾ yard
Backing	5⅞ yards
Batting	72" x 99"

* Amount needed if you don't want to piece your border. If you want to bind your quilt with the same fabric, you can omit the binding yardage when you buy this quantity for your wide border.

Materials for Driftwood	
Finished quilt size: 89" x 104" (queen)	
Color 1 (outer stripes & center square)	2⅝ yards
Color 2 (center stripe & small edges of log cabins)	2⅜ yards
Color 3 (long edges of Log Cabins	1⅞ yards
Narrow border	½ yard
Wide border	2 yards (3*)
Binding	⅞ yard
Backing	8½ yards
Batting	97" x 112"

* Amount needed if you don't want to piece your border. If you want to bind your quilt with the same fabric, you can omit the binding yardage when you buy this quantity for your wide border.

Cutting Chart for Driftwood Finished block size: 9" x 9" (twin)

Fabric	Piece code	# of strips	Strip width	Piece length	# of pieces
Color 1	N	14*	3½"	9½"	54
	C	3	3½"	3½"	27
Color 2	W	7*	3½"	9½"	27
	C	3	3½"	3½"	27
	D	5	3½"	6½"	27
Color 3	D	5	3½"	6½"	27
	E	7	3½"	9½"	27
Narrow border		8	1½"		
Wide border		9	4½"		
Binding		9	2½"		
Batting		72" x 99"			
Backing		2 panels, 40" x 99"			

*Strip piece before cutting to length.

Cutting Chart for Driftwood Finished block size: 7½" x 7½" (queen)

Fabric	Piece code	# of strips	Strip width	Piece length	# of pieces
Color 1	N	24*	3"	8"	120
	C	5	3"	3"	60
Color 2	W	12*	3"	8"	60
	C	5	3"	3"	60
	D	9	3"	5½"	60
Color 3	D	9	3"	5½"	60
	E	12	3"	8"	60
Narrow border		9	1½"		
Wide border		10	6½"		
Binding		10	2½"		
Batting		97" x 112"			
Backing		3 panels, 40" x 97"			

*Strip piece before cutting to length.

All That Jazz!

Made by Nancy Mossbarger
Columbia, Missouri
Quilted by the author, 52" x 64"
(See pages 53-54 for alternate sizes.)

Level of difficulty: Easy
Finished block size: 6" x 6"

All That Jazz!

ALL THAT JAZZ! utilizes the same two blocks as the Driftwood quilts. The differences are in the orientation of the blocks and the widths of the strips in the Stripe blocks.

How much fabric do I need?

Materials for All That Jazz!	
Finished quilt size: 52" x 64" (lap)	
Red	⅞ yard
Black print	¾ yard
White print	1⅛ yards
Narrow border	⅜ yard
Wide border	1 yard (1⅞*)
Binding	⅝ yard
Batting	60" x 72"
Backing	3½ yards

* Amount needed if you don't want to piece your border.

How many blocks do I need to make?

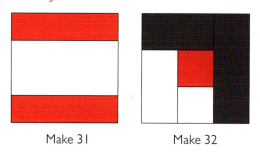

Make 31   Make 32

Making the Stripe and Log Cabin Blocks

1. Construct 31 Stripe blocks according to the instructions on page 8.

2. Construct 32 Log Cabin blocks according to the instructions on page 8.

All That Jazz! Assembly

1. Arrange the blocks in 9 rows of 7 blocks each, orienting them as shown on page 53 to achieve the diagonal design.

What do I need to cut?

Cutting Chart for All That Jazz!			Finished block size: 6" x 6" (lap)		
Fabric	Piece code	# of strips	Strip width	Piece length	# of pieces
Red	N	12*	2"	6½"	62
	C	2	2½"	2½"	32
Black print	D	4	2½"	4½"	32
	E	6	2½"	6½"	32
White print	W	6*	3½"	6½"	32
	C	2	2½"	2½"	32
	D	4	2½"	4½"	32
Narrow border		6	1½"		
Wide border		7	4½"		
Binding		7	2½"		
Batting			60" x 72"		
Backing			2 panels, 40" x 60"		

* Strip piece before cutting to length.

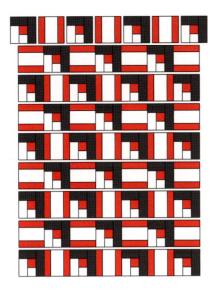

Backing

Piece the backing panels according to the piecing diagram on page 80.

Alternate Sizes

The twin and queen sizes are constructed just like the lap quilt. Twin: 14 rows of 9 blocks each; queen: 14 rows of 12 blocks each.

2. Join the blocks into rows, pressing the seams in each row in opposite directions. Join the rows, carefully matching and pinning the seams. Press all the seams in the same direction.

3. Trim up the edges of your quilt with your long ruler and rotary cutter.

Borders

Add the narrow inner border and the wide outer border following the instructions on page 9.

Materials for All That Jazz!

Finished quilt size: 64" x 94" (twin)

Red	1⅝ yards
Black print	1½ yards
White print	2 yards
Narrow border	½ yard
Wide border	1⅜ yards (2¾*)
Binding	¾ yard
Batting	72" x 102"
Backing	6 yards

* Amount needed if you don't want to piece your border.

Cutting Chart for All That Jazz!   Finished block size: 6" x 6" (twin)

Fabric	Piece code	# of strips	Strip width	Piece length	# of pieces
Red	N	22*	2"	6½"	126
	C	4	2½"	2½"	63
Black print	D	8	2½"	4½"	63
	E	11	2½"	6½"	63
White print	W	11*	3½"	6½"	63
	C	4	2½"	2½"	63
	D	7	2½"	4½"	63
Narrow border		9	1½"		
Wide border		10	4½"		
Binding		10	2½"		
Batting			72" x 102"		
Backing			2 panels, 40" x 102"		

* Strip piece before cutting to length.

Materials for All That Jazz!

Finished quilt size: 82" x 94" (queen)

Red	2⅛ yards
Black print	1⅞ yards
White print	2¾ yards
Narrow border	½ yard
Wide border	1⅜ yards (2¾*)
Binding	¾ yard
Batting	90" x 102"
Backing	9 yards

* Amount needed if you don't want to piece your border.

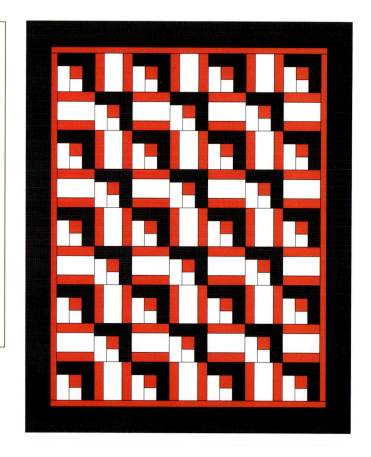

Cutting Chart for All That Jazz!

Finished block size: 6" x 6" (queen)

Fabric	Piece code	# of strips	Strip width	Piece length	# of pieces
Red	N	28*	2"	6½"	168
	C	6	2½"	2½"	84
Black print	D	11	2½"	4½"	84
	E	14	2½"	6½"	84
White print	W	14*	3½"	6½"	84
	C	6	2½"	2½"	84
	D	11	2½"	4½"	84
Narrow border		9	1½"		
Wide border		10	4½"		
Binding		10	2½"		
Batting		90" x 102"			
Backing		3 panels, 40" x 102"			

* Strip piece before cutting to length.

Winding River

Made and quilted by the author, 30" x 38"

(See page 57 for an alternate size.)

Level of difficulty: Easy

Finished block size: 3" x 4"

Winding River

Winding River is an easy wall quilt that goes together quickly.

How much fabric do I need?

Materials for Winding River	
Finished quilt size: 30" x 38" (wall)	
Background fabric for Snow Geese	½ yard
Corners & middle stripes	⅝ yard
Outer stripes	½ yard
Narrow border	¼ yard
Wide border	½ yard
Binding	⅓ yard
Backing	1⅜ yards
Batting	38" x 46"

How many blocks do I need to make?

Make 32   Make 32   or   Make 32   Make 32

Making the Stripe and Snow Goose Blocks

1. Construct 32 Stripe blocks according to the instructions on page 8.

2. Construct 32 Snow Goose blocks according to the instructions on page 8.

Winding River Assembly

1. Arrange the blocks in rows as shown on page 57.

What do I need to cut?

Cutting Chart for Winding River				Finished block size: 3" x 4" (wall)	
Fabric	Piece code	# of strips	Strip width	Piece length	# of pieces
Background for Snow Geese	A	4	3½"	4½"	32
Outer stripes	N*	8	1½"	4½"	64
Corners for Snow Geese	B	4	2½"	2½"	64
Middle stripes	W*	4	1½"	4½"	32
Narrow border		4	1⅛"		
Wide border		4	3"		
Binding		4	2½"		
Batting			38" x 46"		
Backing			1 panel, 40" x 46"		

*Strip piece before cutting to length.

2. Join the blocks into rows, pressing the seams in each row in opposite directions. Join the rows, carefully matching and pinning the seams. Press all the seams in the same direction.

3. Clean up the edges of your quilt top using your long ruler and rotary cutter, and you're ready to add your borders.

Borders

Add the narrow inner border and the wide outer border following the instructions on page 9.

Backing

The backing for the wall quilt is one unpieced panel.

Alternate Size and Colorway

The lap quilt is made with two colors, but yardage for a three-color version is given as well. It is constructed just like the wall quilt.

WINDING RIVER
58" x 74"
Made and quilted by
Sue Collins, Columbia, Missouri

Materials for Winding River

	2-color	3-color
Finished quilt size: 58" x 74" (lap)		
Background fabric for Snow Geese	1⅝ yards	1⅝ yards
Corners & middle stripes	1¾ yards	1¾ yards
Outer stripes	1¼ yards	1¼ yards
Narrow border	⅜ yard	⅜ yard
Wide border	1⅛ yards	1⅛ yards
Binding	⅔ yard	⅔ yard
Backing	3⅞ yards	3⅞ yards
Batting	66" x 82"	66" x 82"

Note: In 2 color quilt, background and outer stripe fabrics are the same – total 2⅔ yard.

Cutting Chart for Winding River   Finished block size: 6" x 8" (lap)

Fabric	Piece code	# of strips	Strip width	Piece length	# of pieces
Background for Snow Geese	A	8	6½"	8½"	32
Outer stripes	N*	16	2½"	8½"	64
Corners for Snow Geese	B	8	4½"	4½"	64
Middle stripes	W*	8	2½"	8½"	32
Narrow border		7	1½"		
Wide border		8	4½"		
Binding		8	2½"		
Batting		66" x 82"			
Backing		2 panel, 42" x 66"			

*Strip piece before cutting to length.

Four Corners
Made and quilted by the author
53½" x 53½" (See page 62 for an alternate size.)

Level of difficulty: Medium
Technique: On-point construction
Finished block size: 6" x 6"

Four Corners

The Log Cabin, Stripe, and Snow Goose blocks are each made in two different color arrangements and the blocks are set on point. The quilt looks distinctly southwestern when constructed in turquoise and black.

How much fabric do I need?

Materials for Four Corners

Finished quilt size: 53½" x 53½" (lap)	
Black – includes wide border & binding	2⅓ yards
Turquoise – includes narrow border	¾ yard
White	1⅛ yards
Backing	3¼ yards
Batting	62" x 62"

What do I need to cut?

Cutting Chart for Four Corners
Finished block size: 6" x 6" (lap)

Fabric	Piece code	# of strips	Strip width	Piece length	# of pieces
Black	C	3	2½"	2½"	1
	D	3	2½"	4½"	10
	E	3	2½"	6½"	9
	N	2*	2"	6½"	8
	A	3	6½"	6½"	16
	B	1	3½"	3½"	8
Turquoise	C	1	2½"	2½"	8
	D	1	2½"	4½"	8
	N	3*	2	6½"	16
White	C	1	2½"	2½"	9
	W	2*	3½"	6½"	12
	B	3	3½"	3½"	32
	A	1	6½"	6½"	4
	setting triangles	1	11⅜"	11⅜"	4
	corner triangles	1	5¾"	5¾"	2
Narrow border (turquoise)		5	2"		
Wide border (black)		6	4½"		
Binding (black)		6	2½"		
Batting		62" x 62"			
Backing		1 panel, 40" x 62"; 2 panels, 31" x 22"			

* Strip piece before cutting to length.

Patchwork 4 Ways by Kathleen Hulett

How many blocks do I need to make?

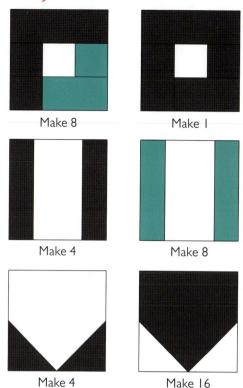

Make 8   Make 1

Make 4   Make 8

Make 4   Make 16

Making the Blocks

1. Construct 9 Log Cabin blocks according to the instructions on page 8 and the block chart above.

2. Construct 12 Stripe blocks according to the instructions on page 8 and the block chart above.

3. Construct 20 Snow Goose blocks according to the instructions on page 8 and the block chart above.

Four Corners Assembly

1. Cut your side and corner setting triangles according to the instructions on page 9 .

2. Lay out your blocks and side setting triangles as shown, repeating the top 4 rows for the lower half of the quilt.

3. Join the blocks into rows, pressing the seams in each row in opposite directions. Join the rows, carefully matching and pinning the seams. Press all the seams in the same direction.

4. Your quilt top will now look like a rough square, although the triangles on the edges are too big and the corners look chopped off.

5. Center a corner triangle on each of the chopped off corners. They won't fit exactly, but don't worry about that just yet. Just sew them on.

6. Clean up the edges of your quilt top using your long ruler and rotary cutter, making sure to leave a 1/4"–3/8" seam allowance beyond the points of your blocks.

Borders

Add the narrow inner border and the wide outer border following the instructions on page 9.

Backing

Piece the backing panels according to the piecing diagram on page 80.

Alternate Size

The smaller FOUR CORNERS quilt is made with the same number of blocks in a smaller size (4½" x 4½" finished).

Materials for Four Corners

Finished quilt size: 40" x 40" (wall)

Black – includes wide border & binding	1⅝ yards
Turquoise – includes narrow border	½ yard
White	1⅜ yards
Backing	1⅜ yards if 44" wide
Batting	44" x 44"

Cutting Chart for Four Corners   Finished block size: 4½" x 4½" (wall)

Fabric	Piece code	# of strips	Strip width	Piece length	# of pieces
Black	C	3	2"	2"	1
	D	3	2"	3½"	10
	E	3	2"	5"	9
	N	2*	2"	5"	8
	A	2	6½"	5"	16
	B	1	3½"	2¾"	8
Turquoise	C	1	2½"	2"	8
	D	1	2½"	3½"	8
	N	2*	2	5"	16
White	C	1	2½"	3"	9
	W	2*	3½"	5"	12
	B	2	3½"	2¾"	32
	A	1	6½"	5"	4
	setting triangles	1	7¾"	7¾"	4
	corner triangles	1	4½"	4½"	2
Narrow border (turquoise)		4	1½"		
Wide border (black)		4	3½"		
Binding (black)		5	2½"		
Batting			44" x 44"		
Backing			1 44" panel of 44" wide fabric		

* Strip piece before cutting to length.

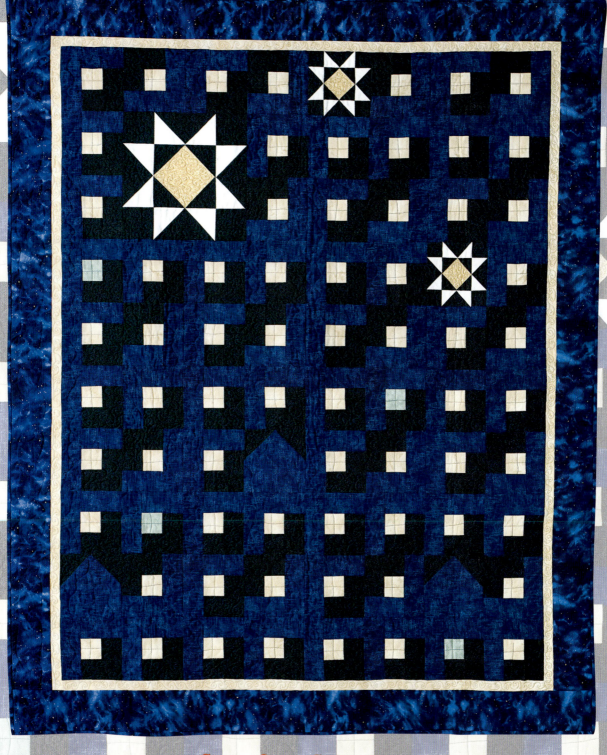

Stars Over Suburbia

Made and quilted by the author,
58" x 70"

Level of difficulty: Easy–medium
Techniques: Insertion of larger block into pattern
Finished block sizes: 6" x 6" and 12" x 12"

Stars Over Suburbia

The Log Cabin, Snow Goose, and Star blocks are all used in this quilt. Look closely and you'll see a few rooftops amongst the lighted windows of nighttime suburbia. You'll notice that a few of the windows are without light. Perhaps the occupants are settled for the night under a nice warm quilt.

How much fabric do I need?

Materials for Stars Over Suburbia	
Finished quilt size: 58" x 70" (lap)	
Blue	1¾ yards
Black	1⅜ yards
Light gold	⅜ yard
Medium gold	¼ yard
Gray green	⅛ yard
White	¼ yard
Narrow border	⅜ yard
Wide border & binding	1¾ yards
Backing	3⅞ yards
Batting	66" x 78"

What do I need to cut?

See the cutting chart on page 65.

How many blocks do I need to make?

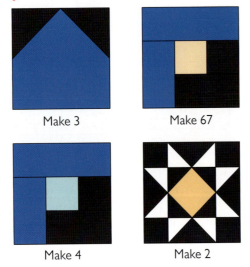

Make 3

Make 67

Make 4

Make 2

Making the Blocks

1. Construct 3 Snow Goose blocks according to the instructions on page 8.

2. Construct 67 Log Cabin blocks according to the instructions on page 8 in the color arrangements shown below.

3. Construct 2 small and 1 large Star blocks according to the instructions on page 7.

Stars Over Suburbia Assembly

1. Arrange the blocks in rows as shown.

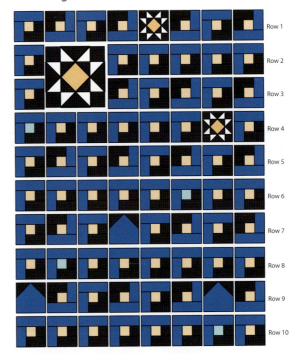

Row 1
Row 2
Row 3
Row 4
Row 5
Row 6
Row 7
Row 8
Row 9
Row 10

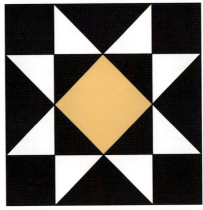

Make 1

Cutting Chart for Stars Over Suburbia — Finished block sizes: 6" x 6", 12" x 12"

Fabric	Piece code	# of strips	Strip width	Piece length	# of pieces
Blue	D	9	2½"	4½"	71
	E	12	2½"	6½"	71
	A	1	6½"	6½"	3
Black	D	14	2½"	4½"	71
	C	14	2½"	2½"	71
	D	2	3½"	6½"	4
	C	2	3½"	3½"	8
	B	2	3½"	3½"	6
	D	2	2"	3½"	8
	C	2	2"	2"	16
Light gold	C	5	2½"	2½"	67
Gray green	C	1	2½"	2½"	4
White	C	1	3½"	3½"	8
	C	1	2"	2"	16
Medium gold (star centers)	B – lg	1	6½"	6½"	1
Trim strip for smaller squares	B – sm	1	3½"	3½"	2
Narrow border		7	1½"		
Wide border		8	4½"		
Binding		8	2½"		
Batting		66" x 78"			
Backing		2 panels: 40" x 66"			

Stars Over Suburbia

2. Join the blocks into rows, pressing the seams in each row in opposite directions.

3. Sew rows 2 and 3 of the Log Cabin blocks together, then join the double row to the large Star block. Join the two Log Cabin blocks to the left of the Star block and add to the Star to complete rows 2 and 3.

4. Join the remaining rows, carefully matching and pinning the seams. Press all the seams in the same direction.

Borders

Add the narrow inner border and the wide outer border following the instructions on page 9.

Backing

Piece the backing panels according to the piecing diagram on page 80.

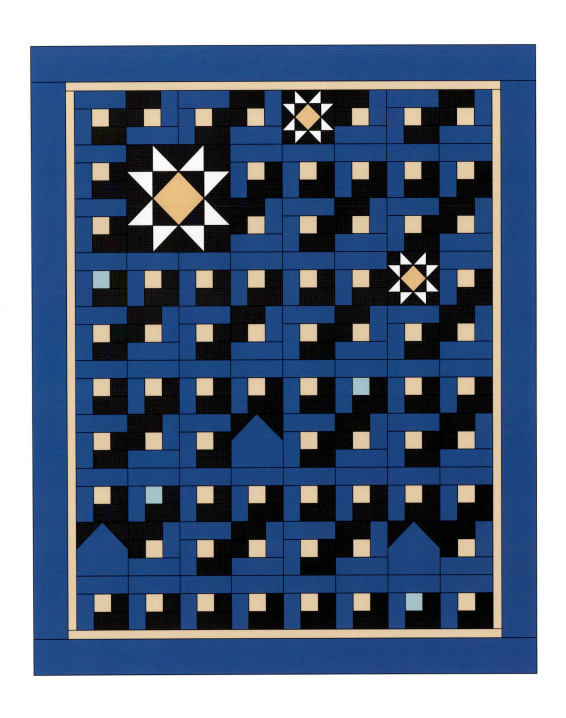

Cottage Garden
Made and quilted by the author, 46" x 59"
(See page 70 for an alternate size.)

Level of difficulty: Medium
Technique: Pieced border
Finished block sizes: 8" x 8", 6" x 8", 4½" x 4½"

Cottage Garden

Can you smell the flowers? An assortment of floral fabrics combines to make a quilt that is reminiscent of a cottage garden pathway.

How much fabric do I need?

Materials for Cottage Garden

Finished quilt size: 46" x 59" (lap)

Dark pink (includes narrow border & binding	1½ yards
Green	½ yard
Light floral	⅜ yard
Background	1⅜ yards
Wide border	⅞ yard (1¾*)
Backing	3¼ yards
Batting	54" x 67"

* Amount needed if you don't want to piece your border.

How many blocks do I need to make?

Make 7 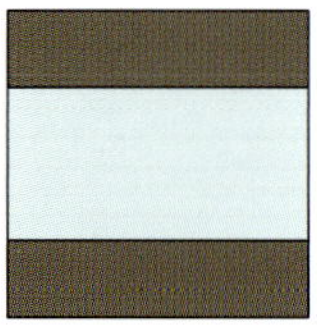   Make 8 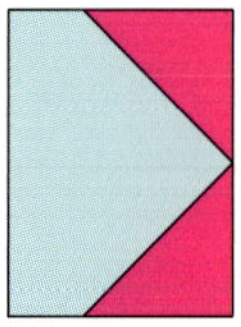   Make 10 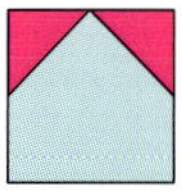   Make 16

Making the Blocks

1. Construct 7 Star blocks according to the instructions on page 7.

2. Construct 8 Stripe blocks according to the instructions on page 8.

3. Construct 10 large and 16 small Snow Goose blocks according to the instructions on page 8.

What do I need to cut?

Cutting Chart for Cottage Garden

Finished block sizes: 8" x 8", 6" x 8", 4½" x 4½" (lap)

Fabric	Piece code	# of strips	Strip width	Piece length	# of pieces
Dark pink	C	4	2½"	2½"	56
	B – lg	3	4½"	4½"	20
	B – sm	2	2½"	2½"	32
Blue	B	1	4½"	4½"	7
	N	4*	2½"	8½"	16
Light floral	W	2*	4½"	8½"	8
Background	C	4	2½"	2½"	56
	D	2	4½"	2½"	28
	A – lg	2	8½"	6½"	10
	A – sm	2	5"	5"	16
Narrow border	dark pink	5	1½"		
Wide border	blue floral	6	4½"		
Binding	dark pink	6	2½"		
Batting			54" x 67"		
Backing			2 panels, 40" x 54"		

* Strip piece before cutting to length

Cottage Garden Assembly

1. Arrange the blocks in rows as shown, including the two rows of the Snow Goose border blocks.

2. Join the blocks into rows, pressing the seams in each row in opposite directions. Join the rows, carefully matching and pinning the seams. Press all the seams in the same direction.

3. Add the narrow inner border and the wide outer border following the instructions on page 9.

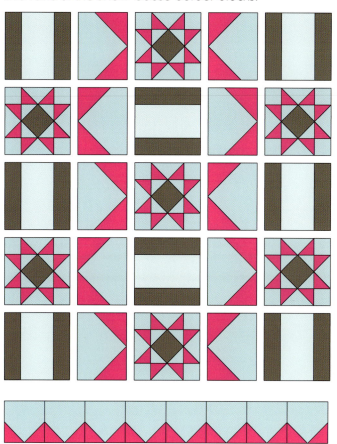

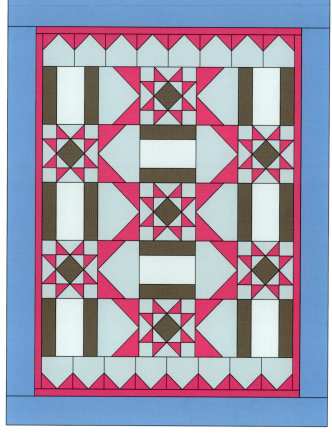

Backing

Piece the backing panels according to the piecing diagram on page 80.

Alternate Size

The queen/king size COTTAGE GARDEN is constructed just like the lap quilt simply by adding more blocks.

Materials for Cottage Garden

Finished quilt size: 102" x 107" (queen)

Dark pink (includes narrow border & binding	5⅛ yards
Green	2⅛ yards
Light floral	1⅜ yards
Background	7¾ yards
Wide border	2 yards (3*)
Backing	10⅛ yards
Batting	110" x 115"

* Amount needed if you don't want to piece your border.

Cutting Chart for Cottage Garden

Finished block sizes: 6" x 8", 8" x 8", 4½" x 4½" (queen)

Fabric	Piece code	# of strips	Strip width	Piece length	# of pieces
Dark pink	C	19	2½"	2½"	304
	B – lg	15	4½"	4½"	132
	B – sm	6	2½"	2½"	76
Green	B	5	4½"	4½"	38
	N	20	2½"	8½"	78
Light floral	W	10	4½"	8½"	39
Background	C	19	2½"	2½"	304
	D	19	4½"	2½"	152
	A – lg	17	8½"	8½"	66
	A – sm	5	4½"	4½"	38
Narrow border	dark pink	10	2"		
Wide border	blue floral	12	5½"		
Binding	dark pink	12	2½"		
Batting		110" x 115"			
Backing		3 panels, 40" x 115"			

* Strip piece before cutting to length.

Cabins in the Stars
Made by the author, 56" x 56"
(See pages 74–77 for alternate sizes.)

Level of difficulty: Medium–Advanced
Finished block size: Varies

Cabins in the Stars

CABINS IN THE STARS was the inspiration for this book. I originally designed it on a free, downloaded demo version of cross-stitch software. I eventually transferred it to EQ5© software where its blocks made their way into the many patterns that fill this book. Making the quilt on a 1" scale (each small square measures 1" x 1") was a challenge, but I love the results, so I think that the challenge was worth it. Instructions and fabric requirements are included for making this quilt in several sizes and scales, so take your pick.

The layout of the quilt is determined by the number of nine-patch Star/Log Cabin/Snow Goose units. The overall size is affected by the scale of the blocks. This version of the quilt is in a 3 x 3 unit layout. Do you see the center Stars in each of the nine units? The smaller wall quilt is a 1 x 1 unit layout made with larger blocks (page 76).

All four blocks are used in this quilt.

What do I need to cut?

How much fabric do I need?

Materials for Cabins in the Stars	
Finished quilt size: 56" x 56" (lap)	
Red	1⅜ yards
Blue	⅞ yard
Green	⅜ yard
Cream	2 yards
Narrow border	¼ yard
Wide border	⅞ yard (1¾*)
Binding	½ yard
Backing	3¾ yards
Batting	64" x 64"

* Amount needed if you don't want to piece your border.

Cutting Chart for Cabins in the Stars
Finished quilt 3 x 3 layout, 1" scale (lap)

Fabric	Piece code	# of strips	Strip width	Piece length	# of pieces
Red	N	10*	1½"	3½"	96
	C	8	1½"	1½"	196
	B	7	2½"	2½"	97
Blue	E	4	1½"	3½"	36
	D	3	1½"	2½"	36
	C	8	1½"	1½"	200
	B	2	2½"	2½"	24
Green	C	8	1½"	1½"	192
Cream	A	5	3½"	4½"	36
	W	5*	2½"	3½"	48
	C	11	1½"	1½"	268
	D	15	1½"	2½"	232
Narrow border		5	1½"		
Wide border		6	4½"		
Binding		6	2½"		
Batting		64" x 64"			
Backing		2 panels: 40" x 64"			

* Strip piece before cutting to length.

How many blocks do I need?

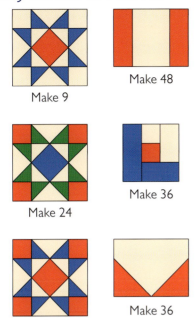

Make 9

Make 48

Make 24

Make 36

Make 16

Make 36

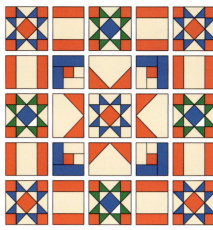

Making the Blocks

The Star blocks are made in various color combinations, so let's break them down to see what kind of units you need.

1. Make all of the Star block units first, then construct the 49 Star blocks from those units according to the instructions on page 7, referring to the block chart above.

2. Construct 48 Stripe blocks according to the instructions on page 8.

3. Construct 36 Log Cabin blocks according to the instructions on page 8.

4. Construct 36 Snow Goose blocks according to the instructions on page 8.

Cabins in the Stars Assembly

Take the quilt assembly one step at a time and it's not nearly as complicated as it looks (though you don't have to tell anyone as they admire your finished quilt!).

1. First make the nine-patch Star units with the Star, Log Cabin, and Snow Goose blocks.

2. Next make the sashing units and sashing rows with the Stripe and Star blocks. Press as you go, matching your seams carefully. Press seam allowances in the opposite direction of the nine-patch Star units so that your quilt top will lie flat when it is complete.

Make 3

Make 4

3. Join the sashing units and nine-patch Star units into rows, then join with the sashing rows to complete the top.

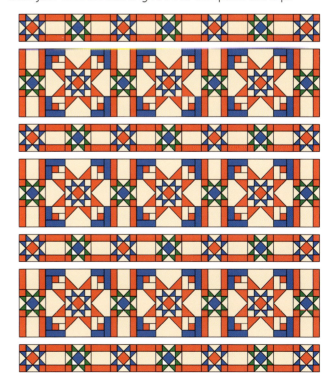

Cabins in the Stars

Borders

Add the narrow inner border and the wide outer border following the instructions on page 9.

Backing

Piece the backing panels according to the piecing diagram on page 80.

Alternate Sizes and Colorway

I've included the requirements for two additional sizes for the 3 x 3 layout of CABINS IN THE STARS. The number of blocks to make is the same as for the 1" scale version (page 72).

Materials for Cabins in the Stars

Finished quilt size: 79" x 79" (full/queen)

Red	2¼ yards
Blue	1½ yards
Green	⅝ yard
Cream	3⅝ yards
Narrow border	⅜ yard
Wide border	1⅛ yards (2⅜*)
Binding	¾ yard
Backing	5⅛ yards
Batting	87" x 87"

* Amount needed if you don't want to piece your border.

Cutting Chart for Cabins in the Stars — Finished quilt 3 x 3 layout, 1½" scale (full/queen)

Fabric	Piece code	# of strips	Strip width	Piece length	# of pieces
Red	N	12*	2"	5"	96
	C	10	2"	2"	196
	B	9	3½"	3½"	97
Blue	E	5	2"	5"	36
	D	4	2"	3½"	36
	C	10	2"	2"	200
	B	3	3½"	3½"	24
Green	C	10	2"	2"	192
Cream	A	6*	5"	6½"	36
	W	6	3½"	5"	48
	C	14	2"	2"	268
	D	22	2"	3½"	232
Narrow border		8	1½"		
Wide border		8	4½"		
Binding		9	2½"		
Batting		87" x 87"			
Backing		2 panels, 44" x 87"			

* Strip piece before cutting to length.

Materials for Cabins in the Stars

Finished quilt size: 102" x 102" (king)

Red	3⅞ yards
Blue	2¼ yards
Green	⅞ yard
Cream	6¼ yards
Narrow border	½ yard
Wide border	1⅝ yards (3*)
Binding	⅞ yard
Backing	9¾ yards
Batting	110" x 110"

* Amount needed if you don't want to piece your border.

Cutting Chart for Cabins in the Stars

Finished quilt 3 x 3 layout, 2" scale (king)

Fabric	Piece code	# of strips	Strip width	Piece length	# of pieces
Red	N	16*	2½"	6½"	96
	C	13	2½"	2½"	196
	B	13	4½"	4½"	97
Blue	E	6	2½"	6½"	36
	D	5	2½"	4½"	36
	C	13	2½"	2½"	200
	B	3	4½"	4½"	24
Green	C	12	2½"	2½"	192
Cream	A	9	6½"	8½"	36
	W	8*	4½"	6½"	48
	C	17	2½"	2½"	268
	D	29	2½"	4½"	232
Narrow border		10	1½"		
Wide border		12	4½"		
Binding		11	2½"		
Batting		110" x 110"			
Backing		3 panels, 40" x 110"			

* Strip piece before cutting to length.

Cabins in the Stars

Made by the author, 35" x 35"

Here is the one-unit quilt in an alternate colorway and two size options—1½" and 2" scale. See if you can find the block that is turned wrong in this quilt. I found it after I'd already quilted it.

The 1 x 1 layout is constructed in the same way as the 3 x 3 arrangement with only one nine-patch Star/Log Cabin/ Snow Goose unit and 4 cornerstone blocks.

Materials for Cabins in the Stars

Finished quilt size: 35" x 35" (wall)

Green	½ yard
Rust	⅜ yard
Gold	¼ yard
Beige	⅝ yard
Narrow border	¼ yard
Wide border	½ yard
Binding	⅜ yard
Backing	1¼ yards
Batting	39" x 39"

Cutting Chart for Cabins in the Stars
Finished quilt 1 x 1 layout, 1½" scale (wall)

Fabric	Piece code	# of strips	Strip width	Piece length	# of pieces
Green	N	2	2"	5"	16
	C	3	2"	2"	48
	B	1	3½"	3½"	9
Rust	E	1	2"	5"	4
	D	1	2"	3½"	4
	C	3	2"	2"	56
Gold	C	2	2"	2"	28
	D	2	2"	3½"	28
Beige	C	1	2"	2"	20
	W	1*	3½"	5"	8
	D	2	3½"	2"	12
	B		3½"	3½"	12
	A	1	5"	6½"	4
Narrow border		4	1½"		
Wide border		4	3½"		
Binding		4	2½"		
Batting		39" x 39"			
Backing		1 panel, 39" x 39"			

* Strip piece before cutting to length.

The number of blocks needed for each size is the same. You'll have 4 extra Star center units that will be used as cornerstones in the border.

Materials for Cabins in the Stars

Finished quilt size: 46" x 46" (lap)

Green	¾ yard
Rust	⅜ yard
Gold	⅜ yard
Beige	1⅛ yards
Narrow border	¼ yard
Wide border	¾ yard
Binding	½ yard
Backing	2½ yards
Batting	50" x 50"

Cutting Chart for Cabins in the Stars

Finished quilt 1 x 1 layout, 2" scale (lap)

Fabric	Piece code	# of strips	Strip width	Piece length	# of pieces
Green	N	3*	2½"	6½"	16
	C	3	2½"	2½"	48
	B	2	4½"	4½"	9
Rust	E	1	2½"	6½"	4
	D	1	2½"	4½"	4
	C	4	2½"	2½"	56
Gold	C	2	2½"	2½"	28
	D	3	2½"	4½"	28
Beige	C	2	2½"	2½"	20
	W	2	4½"	6½"	8
	D	2	2½"	4½"	12
	A	1	6½"	8½"	4
	B	2	4½"	4½"	12
Narrow border		4	1½"		
Wide border		5	4½"		
Binding		6	2½"		
Batting			54" x 54"		
Backing			1 panel, 40" x 54" & 2 panels, 15" x 27"		

* Strip piece before cutting to length.

Leftovers

What do I do with all of those leftover triangles?

By now, you may be wondering what to do with all those triangles that you have cut off and saved in the process of making your quilts. Remember, I told you not to throw them out. You did save them, didn't you?

I have found that if the triangles come from anything that started out smaller than 2½", they are smaller than what I like to use, but feel free to give it a try!

AROUND THE CORNER was made from triangles that were left over from a scrappy Gaggle quilt. I did have to add a few extra triangles and fabrics from my stash for the sashings and borders.

After saving all the triangles that were created by making many of the quilts in this book and by harvesting a few from fellow quilters, I also made LEFTOVERS, a bed-size quilt using one of my favorite blocks. I also raided my stash of light neutral fabrics for the alternate blocks.

Here are some other ideas for you that will make nice pillows, wallhangings, or baby quilts. Use your imagination and you're sure to come up with more possibilities.

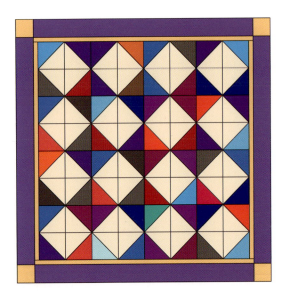

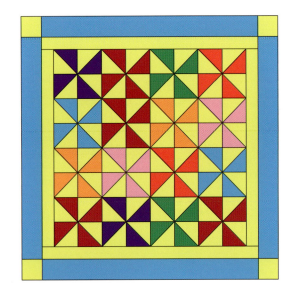

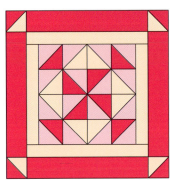

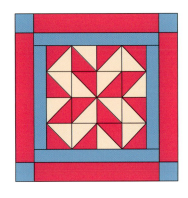

AROUND THE CORNER
Made by the author, 45" x 45"

LEFTOVERS
Made by the author, 91" x 91"

The Three Bs – Backing, Batting & Binding

Once your quilt top is assembled, it is time to consider finishing.

Backing

The dimensions of both the backing and batting materials for your quilt should be 4–8" larger than your quilt top. Smaller quilts do fine with just 4" extra, but if your quilt is larger than 45", it is best to allow the greater amount. For example, if your quilt is 50" x 60", your backing and batting need to be 58" x 68". Not only does this allow for some "pulling up" during quilting, it also provides a margin for error when making your quilt sandwich. Centering the quilt top on the backing and batting can be tricky, and a bit of extra fabric around the edges can help make the process much easier.

The quilts in this book all specify the yardage you will need for your quilt and assume 40" usable fabric width unless specified otherwise. If you buy fabric that is 108" wide, made especially for quilt backs, buy according to your quilt dimensions plus eight inches.

Backing your quilt

If you need 40" or less in width, as is the case with many baby quilts and some wall quilts, you have it easy. Simply cut a length of fabric four inches longer than your quilt top and your backing is ready to use.

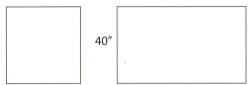

Joining two backing panels

If your quilt is more than 40" wide, you will need to piece your backing. As long as the length you need is less than 80", you can use two panels of fabric, sewn side by side. Take the width of your quilt plus 8" and double it to obtain the length of fabric you will need. Cut or tear your fabric in half and sew the two halves together, side-by-side. Press the resulting seam allowance open. Your quilt back will have a seam going across the middle of your quilt.

When two panels are not enough

If your quilt is very large, as with a queen- or king-size, you may need three lengths of fabric for the backing. For example, if your quilt is 100" x 120", you can use three lengths of 108" long, to back your quilt. Sew them together as shown to obtain the needed size for your backing. The seams will go across the width of your quilt.

Creative backing

Sometimes, your quilt may be just slightly larger than what a single panel of fabric will back. In that case, you can be a bit more creative with piecing your backing and in the process, use less fabric. You will, however, create extra seams in your backing fabric. If this is not a problem for you, go right ahead and do it. Use a 40" width of fabric, then another 40" wide piece is split and sewn end-to-end to cover the remainder of the back. This would work well with a quilt measuring 60" or less in width.

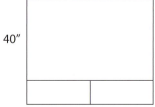

If you have a number of large chunks of coordinating fabrics, but none large enough by itself for a backing, it can be fun to piece them together into a colorful backing. Quilting is all about creativity, so if it looks good, it's right.

Joining your backing panels.

I used to always join my backing panels with a ½" or so seam, and this is quite acceptable. However, a member of my quilt group recently showed me a technique for sewing backing panels together that results in a sturdier seam that lays itself open with little effort. I now prefer it.

To make this type of seam, layer the two backing panels with right sides together and edges even. Fold and press the edge of the top panel down about ½".

Sew close to the folded edge.

The resulting seam allowance will naturally want to open. Press.

Batting

As with the backing, your batting should be 4"–8" longer and wider than your quilt top.

Batting comes in various widths and seldom needs to be pieced if bought for a specific quilt. Some shops sell batting by the yard as well as in prepackaged sizes. Look around at the selection at your local fabric shop and choose a batting that will be of adequate size for your quilt.

If you plan to make many smaller quilts, it can be more economical to purchase a king-size package of batting that can then be cut to use for several quilts. I like to watch for sales and stock up.

Before assembling your quilt sandwich, it is helpful to unfold the batting and let it relax overnight. This helps the wrinkles to soften and makes it easier to smooth out your quilt as you layer it. Cotton battings can be lightly pressed to ease wrinkles out and I recommend this if the batting is heavily creased.

Putting It All Together
(or, Time to Make the Quilt Sandwich)

It's the moment you've been waiting (and working) for. Your quilt top is completed, trimmed, and pressed. Your backing is pieced, ironed, and ready, and your batting is nicely relaxed. (Nobody wants a tense batting, do they?)

Perhaps the most difficult part of the process can be finding an area large enough to lay out your quilt. Once you have located space where you can not only lay the quilt out flat but also maneuver around it, you are ready to go.

I like to use quilt-basting spray to hold my quilt sandwich together. Lay the backing right-side down and smooth it out. If you can pin, clip, or tape it down around the edges, it will resist bunching up as you add the other layers. I use several large, flattened boxes on my basement floor as a work surface and tack the quilt back to the boxes with straight pins. You can also anchor it directly to a carpet. Make sure you have something under the edges to catch any over-spray. It gets a bit sticky!

Next, layer the batting on top of the backing and smooth it out. Then do the same with the quilt top, right-side up. Once you have centered the layers and have the wrinkles smoothed out, you are ready to spray your quilt. Unless your quilt is very small, it helps to enlist the aid of fellow quilters in the process. They'll likely be glad to have your help in the future when it's their turn.

Grasping the corners of one end of the quilt top and batting, fold them back halfway onto the other half of the quilt. Spray the backing with basting spray, according to the directions on the can. Make sure the area is well ventilated.

Fold just the batting back onto the backing, smoothing from the center out toward the edges, being careful to eliminate wrinkles without stretching the batting. Spray the batting, unfold the quilt top onto the batting, and smooth it from the center without stretching it.

Move to the other half of the quilt and repeat the process, folding the top and batting over the half already sprayed.

Even though the quilt is secured with basting spray, I still prefer to pin it in a few places just to be sure. Bent safety pins are ideal for this, but straight pins or regular safety pins will do. Just be careful not to distort your quilt as you pin it and don't stick yourself with those straight pins (ouch!).

Once you have your quilt sandwich secured, you are ready to do the quilting, according to whatever method you prefer. When your quilting is completed, you will be ready to bind your quilt.

Binding

The quilts in this book all call for a binding made from strips of fabric cut 2½" wide. This yields a finished binding that is approximately ½" wide.

Preparing the binding strips

Cut the required number of strips for your binding and sew them together, using diagonal seams, just as you did when you pieced long borders (page 9). If you do not plan to use your binding right away, wrap it around a tube or magazine to keep it from wrinkling.

Sewing the binding to the quilt

Use your long ruler, rotary cutter, and mat to trim the edges and square the corners of your quilt sandwich.

Place the raw edges of your binding even with raw edge of the right side of your quilt and sew with a ¼" seam. Begin sewing several inches from the beginning of the binding strip. A walking foot is helpful when sewing your binding to your quilt.

There are two methods that I like to use. Feel free to use whichever method you prefer.

Binding Method 1 – Fold one end of your binding strip diagonally. Press.

Trim the fold to ¼".

Fold your binding strip in half, lengthwise, with wrong sides together, and press.

Begin sewing the binding to your quilt about 2"–3" from the angled end of the binding.

When you reach the point where you began, tuck the end into the angled end you began with and finish sewing.

Binding Method 2 – Begin sewing your folded, pressed binding around the quilt, starting several inches from the end of the binding and stopping several inches before

you reach the point where you began. Remove your quilt from the machine.

Measure the width of the folded binding. (If you use the recommended 2½" strips, it will be 1¼".) Overlap the ends of the binding and trim so that there is an overlap equal to the width of the folded binding.

Align the binding ends, right sides together and perpendicular to each other.

Sew a seam diagonally to join them.

Open to check, then trim the seam allowance, fingerpress the seam open, and finish sewing your binding to the quilt.

What do I do at the corners?

Stop sewing about ¼" from the edge of your quilt and remove the quilt from the machine. Fold the binding straight up, creating a 45-degree angle fold, keeping the outer edge even with the edge of the quilt.

Fold the binding downward, keeping its edge even with the quilt edge.

Resume sewing with a ¼" seam.

Now for the handwork! – This is the point where you can sit and work on your quilt while watching your favorite movie or TV show (out of one eye, of course). Fold the binding around to the back of your quilt and hand stitch it with thread that matches the binding. Use an invisible stitch.

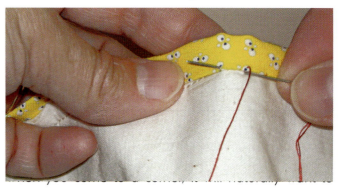

When you come to a corner, it will naturally want to miter itself, but may be a bit uneven. Coax it into the correct position and continue sewing.

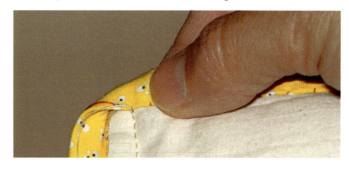

I like to take an extra stitch at the corners to make sure they are secure.

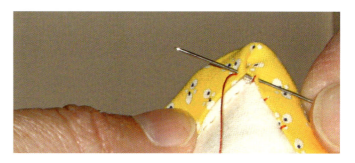

Labels

The Finishing Touch – don't forget to label your quilt.

Your quilt is complete. You've worked hard on it and it's ready to show off. But there is one more little detail to attend to. The label! Years from now, you don't want someone to see the quilt and wonder where it came from or worse yet, see it yourself and wonder when you made it! So label it on the back.

You can do something as simple as using a permanent marker directly on the backing, or something as complex as making a fabric label and appliquéing it onto your quilt. You could even embroider the information onto the binding before you sew it on if you're really ambitious! Whatever you choose, make sure you take credit for your creation. You've earned the right!

And congratulations!

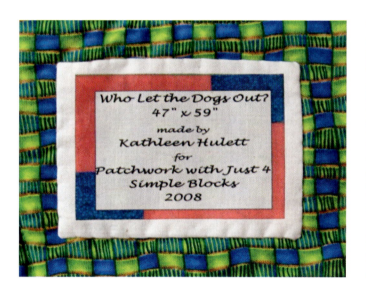

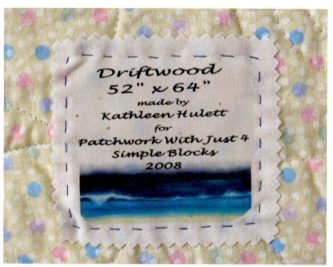

The Math of Quilting

For many, math is scary. When it comes to quilting, your math skills can really come into play. Imagine that you have just found the perfect quilt pattern...almost...okay, not quite. You love the pattern, but it's just not the size you want. You could just keep looking until you find another pattern or you could resize the almost perfect pattern that you just found. "Oh, no I can't," you say. Yes, you can! It's really not as difficult as it sounds. There are two ways to do it. Either change the number of blocks or change the size of the blocks. You can even do both!

That's where this section of the book is useful. In it, you'll discover tools to make the math less of a nightmare and more of a joy— or at least make it tolerable. Play with the patterns in this book and have fun changing things around by using the following tools and examples.

Resizing Your Blocks

What if you like the way the quilt looks with the number of blocks already in it but you don't like the size? You can resize the quilt by making the blocks larger or smaller.

Let's assume that your pattern makes a 6" x 6" block and you want to make 9" x 9" blocks. You want a block 1½ times its original size. The pattern tells you to cut 2½" squares. What size would you need to cut to make the larger block?

You need to keep in mind that the size you cut includes a seam allowance of ¼" all around. That remains constant, no matter what size your pieces are. If you try to resize the pieces without taking the seam allowance into account, your pieces will not turn out right, as you'll be changing the size of the seam allowance along with the piece size.

So, first you need to subtract the seam allowance. Thus, a 2½" x 2½" piece would be 2" x 2". A 2½" x 4½" piece would be 2" x 4". Now, you are ready to increase the size of your pieces by a factor of 1½ (1.5). Do this by multiplying each dimension by 1.5. Your 2" square becomes a 3" square and your 2" x 4" piece becomes 3" x 6".

But you're not done yet. Now, add the seam allowance back in, yielding pieces that are 3½" x 3½" and 3½" x 6½". Using those pieces will yield a block that is 1½ times larger than your original block.

If you prefer not to do the math yourself, the following chart has the changes figured for you for dimensions from 1" to 10½", changing them in size by factors of 0.5–1.5 (½–1½).

Resizing Factors for Block Dimensions (in inches)

Starting Size	Resizing Factor			
	½	¾	1¼	1½
1	3/4	7/8	1 1/8	1 1/4
1¼	7/8	1 1/16	1 7/16	1 5/8
1½	1	1 1/4	1 3/4	2
1¾	1 1/8	1 7/16	2 1/16	2 3/8
2	1 1/4	1 5/8	2 3/8	2 3/4
2¼	1 3/8	1 13/16	2 11/16	3 1/8
2½	1 1/2	2	3	3 1/2
2¾	1 5/8	2 3/16	3 5/16	3 7/8
3	1 3/4	2 3/8	3 5/8	4 1/4
3¼	1 7/8	2 9/16	3 15/16	4 5/8
3½	2	2 3/4	4 1/4	5
3¾	2 1/8	2 15/16	4 9/16	5 3/8
4	2 1/4	3 1/8	4 7/8	5 3/4
4¼	2 3/8	3 5/16	5 3/16	6 1/8
4½	2 1/2	3 1/2	5 1/2	6 1/2
4¾	2 5/8	3 11/16	5 13/16	6 7/8
5	2 3/4	3 7/8	6 1/8	7 1/4
5¼	2 7/8	4 1/16	6 7/16	7 5/8
5½	3	4 1/4	6 3/4	8
5¾	3 1/8	4 7/16	7 1/16	8 3/8
6	3 1/4	4 5/8	7 3/8	8 3/4
6¼	3 3/8	4 13/16	7 11/16	9 1/8
6½	3 1/2	5	8	9 1/2
6¾	3 5/8	5 3/16	8 5/16	9 7/8
7	3 3/4	5 3/8	8 5/8	10 1/4
7¼	3 7/8	5 9/16	8 15/16	10 5/8
7½	4	5 3/4	9 1/4	11
7¾	4 1/8	5 15/16	9 9/16	11 3/8
8	4 1/4	6 1/8	9 7/8	11 3/4
8¼	4 3/8	6 5/16	10 3/16	12 1/8
8½	4 1/2	6 1/2	10 1/2	12 1/2
8¾	4 5/8	6 11/16	10 13/16	12 7/8
9	4 3/4	6 7/8	11 1/8	13 1/4
9¼	4 7/8	7 1/16	11 7/16	13 5/8
9½	5	7 1/4	11 3/4	14
9¾	5 1/8	7 7/16	12 1/16	14 3/8
10	5 1/4	7 5/8	12 3/8	14 3/4
10¼	5 3/8	7 13/16	12 11/16	15 1/8
10½	5 1/2	8	13	15 1/2
10¾	5 5/8	8 3/16	13 5/16	15 7/8

Changing the Number of Blocks

Suppose you are making 8" x 8" blocks and you want to make a queen-size quilt. How do you know how many blocks you will need to make the quilt that size? The following charts can help.

Since a queen-sized bed is about 60" wide by 80" long, you will want to make your quilt about 80" x 90", which gives you a 10" drop on three sides of the bed. If you do not want borders or sashing, use the first chart. Look at the headings across the top of the chart to find the 8" block size. Look down that column until you find the width you want—in this case, 80". To make a quilt 80" wide, it will take 10 blocks across. For the length, you would need 11 or 12 blocks. Multiplying 10 by either 11 or 12, you find that you need to make either 110 or 120 blocks for your quilt, respectively.

What if I want borders?

Let's assume that you want your quilt to include two borders—a 1" finished and a 4" finished border. You still do not plan to include sashing between your blocks, so the following chart will be the one you will use.

Look across the top, in the same way as with the previous chart, and you will find that in order to make an approximately 80" x 90" quilt, you will need to make your quilt 9 x 10 blocks (or 90 blocks, total). This will actually make your quilt 82" x 90", but that is close enough. If you prefer it to be an exact 80" x 90", you can always modify your border widths just a bit, using 3" borders on the sides, instead of 4".

Quilt Size Charts
How many blocks? What size quilt?

No border or sashing								
Block size/inches	4	5	6	7	8	9	10	11	12
Blocks/row									
1	4	5	6	7	8	9	10	11	12
2	8	10	12	14	16	18	20	22	24
3	12	15	18	21	24	27	30	33	36
4	16	20	24	28	32	36	40	44	48
5	20	25	30	35	40	45	50	55	60
6	24	30	36	42	48	54	60	66	72
7	28	35	42	49	56	63	70	77	84
8	32	40	48	56	64	72	80	88	96
9	36	45	54	63	72	81	90	99	108
10	40	50	60	70	80	90	100	110	120
11	44	55	66	77	88	99	110	121	
12	48	60	72	84	96	108	120		
13	52	65	78	91	104	117			

No sashing, 1" & 4" borders								
Block size/inches	4	5	6	7	8	9	10	11	12
Blocks/row									
1	14	15	16	17	18	19	20	21	22
2	18	20	22	24	26	28	30	32	34
3	22	25	28	31	34	37	40	43	46
4	26	30	34	38	42	46	50	54	58
5	30	35	40	45	50	55	60	65	70
6	34	40	46	52	58	64	70	76	82
7	38	45	52	59	66	73	80	87	94
8	42	50	58	66	74	82	90	98	106
9	46	55	64	73	82	91	100	109	118
10	50	60	70	80	90	100	110	120	130
11	54	65	76	87	98	109	120		
12	58	70	82	94	106	118			
13	62	75	88	101	114	127			

What if I want to use sashing between the blocks?

The following charts are for quilts with 1" finished sashing between the blocks, either with or without borders. Use them the same way as the first two charts.

If you want to include more than the two borders specified in the charts, simply add the width of those borders twice (to include both sides of the quilt). For example, if you want another 1" border, add 2" to the measurement given in the chart.

With 1" sashing, including sashed border									
Block size/inches	4	5	6	7	8	9	10	11	12
Blocks/row									
1	6	7	8	9	10	11	12	13	14
2	11	13	15	17	19	21	23	25	27
3	16	19	22	25	28	31	34	37	40
4	21	25	29	33	37	41	45	49	53
5	26	31	36	41	46	51	56	61	66
6	31	37	43	49	55	61	67	73	79
7	36	43	50	57	64	71	78	85	92
8	41	49	57	65	73	81	89	97	105
9	46	55	64	73	82	91	100	109	118
10	51	61	71	81	91	101	111	121	131
11	56	67	78	89	100	111	122		
12	61	73	86	97	109	121			
13	66	79	93	105	118				

With 1" sashing, 1" & 4" borders									
Block size/inches	4	5	6	7	8	9	10	11	12
Blocks/row									
1	16	17	18	19	20	21	22	23	24
2	21	23	25	27	29	31	33	35	37
3	26	29	32	35	38	41	44	47	50
4	31	35	39	43	47	51	55	59	63
5	36	41	46	51	56	61	66	71	76
6	41	47	53	59	65	71	77	83	89
7	46	53	60	67	74	81	88	95	102
8	51	59	67	75	83	91	99	107	115
9	56	65	74	83	92	101	110	119	128
10	61	71	81	91	101	111	121		
11	66	77	88	99	110	121			
12	71	83	95	107	119				
13	76	89	102	115					

How much fabric do I need for the blocks?

Calculating the amount of fabric you need to buy does not have to be difficult. There are probably other methods, but this is the one I use and it seems to work out well.

For our example, we'll use 1 unit of the Cabins in the Stars pattern with the 1 block layout on a 2" scale.

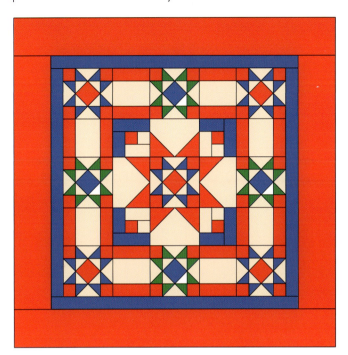

Step 1: Total up the identical blocks in the quilt.

Example:

> Blue/red Star with light corners: 1
>
> Blue/red Star with red corners: 4
>
> Green/blue Star: 4
>
> Snow Geese: 4
>
> Log Cabin: 4
>
> Stripe: 8

Step 2: Count your pieces per block.

List the quantity of each type of piece that you will need for one block. Add ½" to each measurement to allow for the ¼" seam allowance for each piece.

Example:

For the blue/red Star with red corners you will need the pieces specified in the following chart.

Repeat this process for the remaining blocks.

Step 3: Count your blocks.

Multiply the pieces you need per block by the number of blocks you need for the quilt.

Example: Since there are 4 of the blue/red Stars with red corners in this quilt, you will multiply the number of pieces needed per block by 4.

Repeat this step for the remaining blocks in the quilt.

Calculate pieces needed per block

Color	Location of piece	Finished Size	Size to Cut	How many
Red	Star center	4" x 4"	4½" x 4½"	4
Red	Corners	2" x 2"	2½" x 2½"	4
Light	Star center	2" x 2"	2½" x 2½"	4
Light	Flying Geese	2" x 4"	2½" x 4½"	4
Blue	Flying Geese	2" x 2"	2½" x 2½"	8

Calculate pieces needed per quilt

Color	Size to Cut	How many per block?	Number of blocks in quilt	Number of pieces needed
Red	4½" x 4½"	1		4
Red	2½" x 2½"	4		16
Light	2½" x 2½"	4	4	16
Light	2½" x 4½"	4		16
Blue	2½" x 2½"	8		32

The Math of Quilting

Step 4: Calculate the number of strips of fabric to cut.

I like to assume a 40" usable fabric width for most calculations. Although your fabric may be wider, this measurement allows for shrinkage prior to cutting and for variations in widths. Better to have a bit extra length than not enough.

Group pieces of the same color by their widths, if any are the same width. In our example, the light colored pieces are all 2½" wide, but there are no other duplicate widths. If we had repeated the calculations for the rest of the quilt, there would be other duplicates that we could then combine as we calculate our needs.

Example:
Widths needed:

Red: 4½"   4 pieces, 4½" long
       2½"   16 pieces 2½" long
Light: 2½"   16 pieces 2½" long and 16 pieces 4½" long
Blue: 2½"   32 pieces 2½" long

Step 5: How many pieces can I cut from one strip?

Next, you will need to determine how many pieces you can cut of the needed lengths from one strip of fabric. The lengths you will need are 4½" and 2½". Dividing 40" by these numbers, you'll find that you can cut eight 4½" pieces or sixteen 2½" pieces from one strip. You can use the following chart, which has these calculations already done for you.

Example:
Red: Since you only need four red pieces that are 4½" x 4½", one strip will suffice. You need 16 pieces of 2½" x 2½". Since you can get 16 from one strip, one strip will do for this group of pieces as well.
Light: For the 16 pieces of 2½" x 2½", you need one strip. For the 16 pieces that are 2½" x 4½" you will need two strips, as you can only cut eight pieces from each strip.
Blue: For the 32 pieces of 2½" x 2½", you will need two strips, cutting 16 pieces from each strip.

Include all of the blocks from your quilt in these calculations, combining like pieces of the same color before determining strip needs.

How many pieces can I cut from one strip?

Length of piece (inches)	# of pieces possible from 40" strip	# of pieces possible from 42" strip
1	40	42
1½	27	28
2	20	21
2½	16	17
3	13	14
3½	11	12
4	10	11
4½	8	9
5	8	8
5½	7	8
6	6	7
6½	6	6
7	5	6
7½	5	6
8	5	5
8½	4	5
9	4	5
9½	4	4
10	4	4

Inch to Yard Equivalents

Inches	Yards	Yards
4½	⅛	0.125
9	¼	0.25
12	⅓	0.33
13½	⅜	0.375
18	½	0.5
22½	⅝	0.625
24	⅔	0.66
27	¾	0.75
31½	⅞	0.875
36	1	1
40½	1⅛	1.125
45	1¼	1.25
48	1⅓	1.33
49½	1⅜	1.375
54	1½	1.5
58½	1⅝	1.625
60	1⅔	1.66
63	1¾	1.75
67½	1⅞	1.875
72	2	2

Step 6: Calculate your yardage requirements.

Total up the strip widths and add 4" to determine how much fabric you will actually need to purchase for your quilt. More than once I have bought fabric according to the exact amount that I needed to cut and ended up back at the fabric store an inch or two short. That extra 4" is well worth it, making up for crooked cuts at the store or shrinkage of the fabric when you prewash it. Use the inch-to-yard equivalent chart to translate the amount you need from inches to yardage amounts. Round up if your amount falls between two yardage amounts.

Example:

You will need

Red: One 4½" strip and one 2½" strip yields 7" of fabric. Add 4" to total 11" of fabric. This is just under ⅓ yard. Allow ⅓ yard of fabric for this quilt.

Light: Three 2½" strips yields 7½" of fabric. Again, ⅓ yard will suffice.

Blue: Two 2½" strips yields 5" of fabric. Adding 4" will total 9" of fabric, which is ¼ yard.

Calculating Borders and Bindings

To calculate the fabric needs for the borders, determine the width of the strips you will need for the desired border width. Do this by adding ½" to the finished width of the border.

The length you need is approximately the total of the four sides of your quilt. If your quilt is larger than 40" on any one side, you will need to allow extra fabric for piecing your border as described in the section on making borders (pages 9–10). When you piece a border using a diagonal seam, you lose some fabric length. You'll need to account for that extra length in order to calculate the number of strips that you'll need. For each seam, add length equal to the width of the strip you'll use.

For example, if you are piecing 4½" wide strips to make a 60" border, you'll actually need 64½" of fabric. Looking at it another way, if you are piecing 4½" strips, two 40" strips will yield a long strip that is only 75½" long (80" minus 4½"). Three 40" strips of 4½" width, pieced together with diagonal seams, will yield a 111" strip (120" minus 9").

Going back to our example of the one unit quilt, the finished quilt is 46" x 46". Before the borders are added it is 36" x 36". Therefore, our first border strips will not need to be pieced. To make a 1" narrow border, we will need four strips, each 1½" wide, for a total of 6" of fabric. Add 4" and round up to ⅓ yard of fabric needed for the first border.

After adding the first set of borders, the quilt will be 38" square, so the first two wider border strips can be made without piecing as well. That means that you will need two strips, 4½" wide each. Once these border strips are sewn on, the remaining sides will be 46" long, necessitating piecing of the remaining two border segments. You will need a total of three more strips, pieced together and cut to obtain the needed length for these two sides. This brings our total to five strips, 4½" wide for the wide border or 22½" of fabric width. Add 4" and round the total to ¾ yard to be sure to have enough fabric.

The worksheet on page 92 will make it easier for you to plan your quilt needs. Feel free to copy the worksheet for your own personal use.

NAME OF QUILT:									
Layout / Scale									
		A	B	C	D	E	F	G	H
Color	Piece code	Pieces needed / block	Blocks / quilts	Total pieces needed (A x B)	Piece width / strip width	Length of piece	How many pieces can I cut from 1 strip?	Number of strips needed (C divided by F)	Inches of fabric needed (D x G)
								TOTAL	
							Buy this much fabric		
								TOTAL	
							Buy this much fabric		
								TOTAL	
							Buy this much fabric		
								TOTAL	
							Buy this much fabric		

		Border width	Length needed	Number of strips needed	Inches of fabric needed
Narrow border					
Narrow border					
Wide border					
Binding					
Backing					
DIMENSIONS					
Quilt without border					
Quilt with border(s)					

Acknowledgments

A number of people have been in the background during the making of this book and the quilts that are shown within.

Many thanks go to friends and family and to my fellow members in the "Nobody's Perfect Quilt Group"—Sue C., Linda, Sue M., Diane, and Nancy—for their ideas and constructive criticism, their never-ending encouragement, and their help with making some of the quilts.

Thanks to those at the fabric stores who were kind enough to offer their opinions as I agonized over choosing just the right fabrics to use in the quilts.

Thanks also to Michael, who graciously proofread the text before I submitted it and helped me with the grammar and punctuation.

A big hug and thanks, also, to my husband, Ron, who has put up with quilts and snippets of thread all over the house for a long time, but has given me nothing but encouragement and support all along the way.

And most of all, thanks to my Lord and Savior, Jesus Christ, for allowing me this opportunity and skill.

Credits

All quilt patterns are original to the author.
Illustrations were made using EQ5 and EQ6 software.
Text and charts were made with Microsoft Office Word 2007 and Microsoft Office Excel 2007.

Resources

Barnes, Cheryl, *Quilting Dot-to-Dot: Patterns for Today's Machine Quilter*, American Quilter's Society in Cooperation with Golden Threads, 2006.
p. 24: Red and Blue CABINS IN THE STARS
p. 93: Purple/Green BUILDING BLOCKS
p. 93: Large 2-color WINDING RIVER (Sue Collins)

Emmerson, Keryn, *Pretty Simple Pantographs*, Barnes Publishing, dba, Golden Threads, Wheaton, IL, 2004.
Chain Link in SURBURBIA
Trumpet Vine in CHRISTMAS BUILDING BLOCKS

EQ5 and EQ6 software, The Electric Quilt Company, Bowling Green, Ohio.

Quilting motifs were obtained from http://www.quiltmaker.com and used with permission of Quiltmaker.com. Copyright Quiltmaker 2007.
Counting Sheep, Quiltmaker issue # 83. ©2003 Primedia Inc., in LITTLE LAMB
Snow Blossom, Quiltmaker issue # 46. ©2001 Primedia Inc., in COTTAGE GARDEN
Antebellum, Quiltmaker issue #77. ©2001 Primedia Inc., in COTTAGE GARDEN
Leaf, Quiltmaker issue #89. ©2003 Primedia Inc., in SNOW COTTAGE GARDEN
Sunburst, Quiltmaker issue #84. ©2003 Primedia Inc., in SNOW GOOSE GAGGLE
Swirl, Quiltmaker issue #89. ©2004 Primedia Inc., in DRIFTWOOD

About the Author

Kathleen Hulett

I began quilting several years ago and have learned quite a lot from what I have read, sewn, and gleaned from fellow quilters. I very much enjoy designing quilts and experimenting with patterns and colors to come up with new designs. Math skills have always been an interest of mine, and I have enjoyed incorporating those skills into this book, in the form of charts, detailed instructions, and worksheets for those who have an interest in designing their own quilts or in modifying existing designs.

I have enjoyed handcrafting since childhood, beginning with sewing doll clothes on my little toy sewing machine. My mother taught me the basics of sewing early on, and I progressed to sewing clothing and yearned to learn quilting, buying up bits of fabric that eventually made their way into a quilt—although not made by me! Later, I began piecing fabric scraps into my first bed-sized quilt before I had learned anything about rotary cutting or chain piecing. That quilt now covers a queen-sized bed. I have since made a number of other quilts that have been given as gifts to friends and family and have adorned my home with unfinished and completed quilts and lots of little thread snippets while making the quilts for this book. God bless my dear husband for his endurance and support throughout the process.

Several years ago, I began meeting weekly with several women to enjoy quilting together. My basement living area has been converted into our quilting studio where 2–4 machines and two cutting boards are in use almost every Friday morning. We call ourselves the "Nobody's Perfect Quilt Group." Our unofficial motto is, "As ye sew, so shall ye rip!" We have several seam rippers that find themselves in use often.

I do not consider myself to be an expert, by any means. I'm sure there is much yet to be learned about quilting. I hope that what I have learned so far and share with you in this book will help you in your enjoyment of quilting.

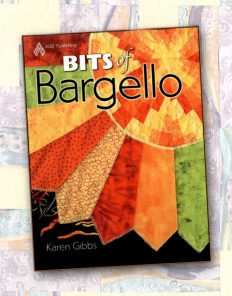
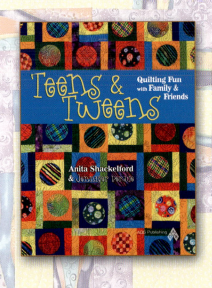

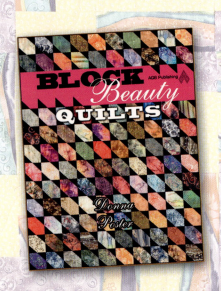
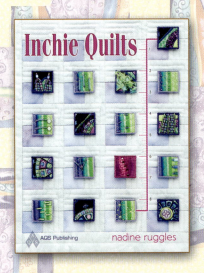
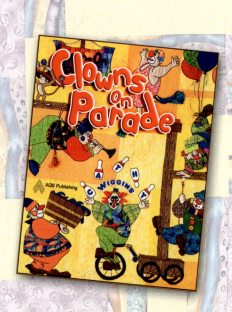